The Four C's of a
BRILLIANT
MARRIAGE

The Secrets to Radiance and Resilience

Charles Humphrey, Jr.

Copyright © 2023 Charles Humphrey, Jr.

All rights reserved.

No part of this publication may be reproduced, distributed, or transmitted in any form or by any means, including photocopying, recording, or other electronic or mechanical methods, without the publisher's prior written permission, except as permitted by U.S. copyright law. For permission requests, contact the publisher.

All scripture quotations are taken from the Holy Bible.

Book Cover by: Juan Roberts, Creative Lunacy (www.CreativeLunacy.com)

Published by: Charles Humphrey, Jr.

1st Edition 2023.

Paperback ISBN

978-1-7323146-1-0

Printed in the United States of America

THE FOUR C's OF A BRILLIANT MARRIAGE
THE SECRETS TO RADIANCE AND RESILIENCE

BY
Charles Humphrey, Jr.

CONTENTS

Dedication ix

Introduction xiii

   Brilliance. xvi

Part I: Formation 1

   Chapter One: Before the Brilliance 1

   Chapter Two: Brilliance from the Bay Area 5

      A Turning Point! 7

      Eighteen Reasons I Should NOT Be Married! 9

      A Second Chance at Love! 12

   Chapter Three: Shopping Around 19

      Wait Just a Minute! 20

      You Better Shop Around! 22

      The Four C's for Diamonds 22

      Who Sets the Standard? 25

      Your "Perfect Partner" Shopping List 26

Part II: Facets 29

   Chapter Four: Facets, Flaws, and Faux Cs 33

      Faux Cs in a Marriage 35

      Cute Together 36

      Charismatic 37

Chemistry 39

Church Affiliation 43

Conflicted Callings? 50

Maintaining the Garden 53

Love is Not Enough 54

Love Needs Some Backup! 57

Chapter Five: What is a Brilliant Marriage? 61

The Four C's of a Brilliant Marriage 64

Chapter Six: Covenant 67

Are You Covenant Ready? 69

The Wedding Vows 71

But What If? 72

Chapter Seven: Communication 79

Say What? 84

Say Something! 85

Say Something (Part 2) 86

You Don't Say? 87

Chapter Eight: Core Values 91

Corporate America Gets It. Why Don't We? 96

God's Core Values 101

Chapter Nine: Counsel 105

Taking Out the Garbage! 107

Who's in Your Ear? 109

Baggage From Self-Counseling? 110

Chapter Ten: Dirty Diamonds and Blurred Brilliance 113

Blurred Brilliance! 114

Brilliance Blockers 120

PART III: FIRE 133

Chapter Eleven: Private Brilliance 137

A Precious Purchased Possession 143

Be the Jeweler in Your Marriage 150

Chapter Twelve: Public Brilliance 157

Chapter Thirteen: A Brilliant Marriage Requires a Brilliant You 167

Being a Brilliant You! 168

Be Willing to Change 170

Be Up for the Challenges 172

Be a Cheerleader for Your Marriage 175

Chapter Fourteen: We're in This Together! 181

Dedication

This book is dedicated to my extraordinary, beautiful, resilient, brilliant wife. From the day we first met on the campus of California State University Northridge, your brilliance was apparent, though I didn't fully grasp its depth then. What captivated me initially was the divine radiance emanating from your heart, a glow that illuminated your interactions with others. Over the years, I witnessed this radiance in various aspects of your life.

During your time in student life and ministry on the college campus, your radiance shone brightly. From our dating days to our wedding, your radiance was undeniable. As you pursued your career and embraced the role of a mother to our incredible daughters, your radiance remained undiminished. Initiating a Bible Study and a church, where you nurtured an environment for others to flourish, showcased your admirable radiance. When you ventured into entrepreneurship, authored two books, and earned your doctorate, your radiance was dazzling. However, every milestone, every accomplishment, demanded more than just radiance; it required resilience.

A beautifully cut diamond doesn't emerge without someone first delving deep into the earth. Excavating the earth isn't glamorous; it's a labor often conducted in obscurity, far from the limelight. It entails getting your hands dirty, navigating challenging terrains, and toiling in confined spaces where workplace injuries might occur unnoticed.

You achieved so much, not just in the spotlight but in the shadows, where your efforts often went unacknowledged. For all your accomplishments achieved and milestones made, you have done much more in obscurity than many will ever know. Sometimes, you didn't receive any credit for digging deep. Sometimes, you did the most work but got the least applause. Yet, and still, all you have been doing since I have known you is sifting through the soil of people's lives so the unearthed diamonds could be brought to the surface. Somehow, you saw the potential for brilliance when others did not. So, you kept digging and sifting. I have seen you sustain workplace injuries. I have seen the dirt under your fingernails. I have seen you work in dark and confined spaces because others put you in a box. I have seen the resilience. Sure, it's easy to be radiant when unveiling diamonds in the bright lights of a jewelry store. But it takes resilience to forge ahead and unearth, polish, and present diamond after diamond so the world can see its glory.

Thank you for demonstrating the consistent effort and skill needed to make "diamonds" in our family and community during our 40 years of friendship, 35 years of marriage, and 20 years of ministry.

I celebrate you.
You make our marriage brilliant!

Acknowledgment

No book goes from "concept" to "critically acclaimed" without some help. To go from mere idea to production, a second set of eyes is necessary. I want to acknowledge and thank some of the "sets of eyes" for their contributions to this literary effort.

Eva Myrick – Simply Affirm (https://www.simplyaffirm.com/)

You encouraged me to tell my story by asking the right questions – even questions I didn't want to answer. Thank you for your encouragement and affirming words.

Samuel Thrinspire ACHI – Thrinspire Media Pub (www.thrinspiremediapub.com)

Thank you for your patience through the process! You were charged with doing the heavy lifting of polishing my words from the pen to the page. Much appreciated!

Richard Smith

Your incredible care for my project and attention to detail was a complete Godsend! Thank you for your friendship and for nurturing this venture as if it were your very own!

Introduction

Congratulations! You have taken your first step toward MARRIAGE BRILLIANCE!

How do I know? Because you have purchased a book that will help you discover the keys to marriage radiance and resilience! Whether you are dating and thinking about marriage, engaged to be married, or already married, this book will help you identify and clarify the necessary elements for your brilliant marriage – one that is both inwardly resilient and outwardly radiant! Now, to be clear, if you want the PERFECT MARRIAGE, this book is not for you. If you want to know the five steps to change your man, you are in the wrong place. If you need the three principles to fix your wife, you may want to look elsewhere. However, if you want to be empowered to build a marriage that matters to you and those around you, this is that book!

Older couples are often asked, "What is the secret to staying married so long?" It's a great question, and here's why – the divorce rate is around 50%, whether the couple is Christian or non-Christian. One source (divorce.com) states that 40% to 50% of married couples file for divorce in the United States. Also, the average length of marriage in the United States is 8.2 years, so people aren't staying together for very long. Even though the lack of marriage longevity begs the question, I think a different question should be considered. The reason is that simply having a long-lasting marriage is good, but it's not God's goal. Some older couples stay in marriages for traditional reasons related to faith or material resources. In some cases, marriages have essentially become an endurance race. Though both parties remain together long-term, they may have become accustomed to enduring disconnection, dissatisfaction, and disappointment. Some hang in there because they feel helpless or hold on when they are not happy. In their minds, "enduring" the relationship is honorable or just the right thing to do." The fairy tale image of the "*...and they lived happily ever after*" marriage is not the goal either. That's because when the story ends, they never show you what the "happily ever after" goal looks like! It is a fantasy that is unattainable.

God's goal for your marriage is BRILLIANCE!

So, I want to challenge you to ask an intentional question about your upcoming or existing marriage – "How can my marriage be BRILLIANT?" I say that God's goal is brilliance because of what the Bible reveals about God, Jesus Christ, and you. The Old Testament often talks about the "glory" of God. That refers to His honor, abundance, reputation, and splendor. The same word, "glory," is used of Jesus on earth as the perfect reflection of God the Father. But in **John 17:22**, Jesus says something quite interesting. He says:

"And the glory which You gave Me I have given them, that they may be one just as We are one."

The word "glory," most often used in the New Testament, refers to an appearance commanding respect, magnificence, and excellence. The "they" He refers to are His followers – that's you and me! God has always intended for His people to reflect His "light" and "glory" on the earth. When it comes to marriage, God continues this theme of sharing His glory, light, and brightness in **Ephesians 5:27** –

> *"...that He might present her to Himself a glorious church, not having spot or wrinkle or any such thing, but that she should be holy and without blemish."*

One version of the Bible says, "He wants to present her to Himself as a "radiant" church, without stain, wrinkle, or any other blemish, but holy and blameless." God wants a radiant bride to match His radiance. And in marriage, the husband is to evoke this radiance in his wife. Since glory or glorious is not a word that is often used, allow me to replace it with a similar word – "Brilliance."

Brilliance

One of the most common and enduring symbols of brilliance is that of a diamond.

The goals for our lives and in our marriages are not survival, persistence, or endurance. It's brilliance! In this book, I want to challenge you to look at your marriage differently. By framing your marriage relationship as a **brilliant diamond**, you will be able to more easily identify the characteristics that either serve to highlight or hijack your potential for marriage brilliance.

In this book, you will be able to:
- Discover the critical characteristics that lead to marriage brilliance,
- Detect the differences between the things that give the appearance of "bling" in marriage but don't lead to long-term brilliance,

- Identify things that can blur or block your marriage's brilliance, and
- Maximize the brilliance in your marriage partner so that you both shine!

You owe it to yourself to discover and put into practice the keys that will make your relationship sparkle! Developing a brilliant marriage doesn't have to take years. It can begin right now with you! So, what are you waiting for? It's your time to shine!

Part I:
Formation

Every diamond is formed.

Long before it was extracted from the earth, cut, polished, and placed in a setting, it was formed. Before it was sold in a high-end store or purchased for an engagement surprise, it was formed. Before it was slipped onto the finger of a new bride-to-be or captured on social media for all to see, it was formed. How long before? An estimated three hundred million years.

According to the Boston Diamond Studio website, every diamond makes an elaborate and arduous journey before becoming a bride's delight. These precious stones were formed in obscurity some 100-200 miles beneath the earth's surface in an environment of intense heat and pressure. Then, through the earth's movement over time, they were pushed upward to the earth's surface to be distributed to diverse locations around the globe. They are most frequently discovered in Australia, Botswana, Canada, Namibia, South Africa, and Russia, accounting for about 80% of the world's diamond supply.

Even when diamonds are found, they can be exceedingly challenging to mine. Over 250 tons of ore are necessary to produce just one carat of rough diamond. This ore goes through several stages of processing to release the diamonds. And even though over 20 million carats are mined each year, only about a quarter of the diamonds mined will be considered gem quality.[1]

The journey of a diamond from formation to a finger-ring is no less complex than your life journey. You, too, were formed. Before you arrived on earth, you were formed in the mind of God

---

[1] BostonDiamondStudio.com

even before the foundation of the world. You were in God's imagination before being formed in His image, according to *Jeremiah 1:5 –*

"Before I formed you in the womb, I knew you, and before you were born, I consecrated you."

During your formation process, just like a diamond, you went through your own dramatic changes before being "pushed to the surface" and birthed.

The same is true of every marriage. Each is destined to endure enormous pressures and encounter a series of dramatic changes to achieve a brilliant result. I intentionally made the connection between a diamond's journey and your journey to remind you of your rarity and value as well as that of your marriage. Without this foundational element, true brilliance will seem elusive. Just as a diamond has intrinsic value, so does your marriage. And just as a diamond is known for both radiance and resilience, your marriage can be both radiant and resilient.

Let's explore the radiant and resilient formation process that can ultimately lead to your marriage's brilliance!

Chapter One

Before the Brilliance

Have you ever seen those before-and-after pictures of movie stars? Yes, the ones that showed them in middle or high school as awkward teenagers. They were fat or skinny, wore thick, horn-rimmed glasses and braces, and looked as if their acne would be a permanent facial feature. The hairstyle of their younger days made you want to question the person who let them leave the house looking like that! But something magical happened between the awkward teenage stage and the teenage heartthrob. Something happened to take them from forgettable to unforgettable and from dorky to dynamic.

They grew. They developed. They honed their skills. They changed to become the people that we love, adore, or idolize, and we pay huge sums to see them do what they do best. In a word, they became BRILLIANT!

Don't get me wrong, they may have always been talented or gifted with the ability to sing, tell jokes, or command the stage in a compelling way. Many always had the seed of the intangible qualities of charisma and stage presence that could not be taught. But they also invested hours, months, and years perfecting their craft and their knowledge. Even though they make what they do look easy now, it didn't all come to them easily.

Most of us have a "marriage picture" in our minds as we approach our time at the altar. That is the "after" version, which is mostly focused on an exquisite ceremony, family and friends supporting and celebrating, and the passion of the honeymoon! But we often think that the "after" picture will come naturally. We fail to consider the impacts of our partners or our personal "before picture" on our marriage. Some of us have troubled pasts, complete with being victims of bullying, abuse, and childhood trauma.

I recently spoke to a college classmate who got married one year before I did. It would be fair to say that her strong church and family upbringing prepared her to be a "good" wife. Or so she thought. What it did not prepare her for was the impact of her partner's family upbringing. She married a man eight years older but newer to the faith than she was. She figured that as long as he was moving forward on his faith journey, any problems encountered would be manageable. She was blessed to know that, along with his newfound faith, he was hardworking, resourceful, and financially stable. During their 20+ years of marriage, they both had careers in academia, owned two late-model cars, owned a large suburban home, and raised four children who excelled academically. To an outsider, everything looked great on paper. What she experienced behind closed doors, however, was anything but great. Over the course of time, she discovered the lingering impacts of his traumatic childhood. This stemmed from an alcoholic and unfaithful father and a mother for whom he could never do enough to please or make her proud. So even though he excelled academically and vocationally, it was never enough for his mom. She simply didn't have the capacity to acknowledge or affirm his hard work and accomplishments.

When my college classmate and her husband eventually went for marriage counseling, her husband's primary complaint was that she was not the "good wife" he had hoped for. It was then she realized that her husband's inability to please his mother was still a real part of his life experience. As a result, her best efforts to please him were never acknowledged or affirmed. Her experience as a wife now mirrored his experience as a son. She would never be considered a good wife if he lived with the trauma of his childhood experience. This is not to imply that she was the perfect wife or without her own set of flaws that contributed to the marital demise. This account is intended to exhibit just one way in which childhood trauma, left unaddressed, can rear its head in a marriage.

Other factors, such as material lack or simply a poverty mentality, can also shape relationship outcomes. On the other end of the spectrum, those who come from affluence and have never wanted anything material can bring a certain level of expectation or entitlement into the partnership. And depending on the generation you were born into, there can be certain expectations and mindsets you bring with you. Just to be clear, this is not just a warning to those who have experienced severe negative influences in their lives. We all have some unhealthy influences or have experienced some challenging childhood, adolescence, or family of origin circumstances that have shaped us. And when two people from varied pasts come together, there is no guarantee of marriage brilliance. My point is that we simply cannot afford to overlook the impact of our "before" as we head into an "after" that we hope will be a brilliant experience with someone else. We need to consider our past rather than assume it will be magically absorbed into the bliss of matrimony.

Chapter Two

Brilliance from the Bay Area

Have you ever been in the presence of greatness and had no idea that you were in the presence of greatness? I think it happens more often than we know. I am not talking about the times you are in the airport or passing through a hotel lobby, and you recognize a movie star or popular entertainer. I am talking about the people you meet every day but don't recognize their greatness. Why? Because they are not yet "great" in the eyes of the media or public when we encounter them. For example, some of us had friends we played sports with on the playground or in our neighborhood. Some of us were taking music or dance classes alongside kids who became incredible creative artists. At the time, we may have thought they were good or exceptionally talented. But when we later saw them play in a World Series or participate in the Olympics, we reflected on how we knew them back in the day.

***

The best basketball player I ever competed against in high school was a kid named Leon Wood. At the time, I knew he was good, but I had no idea he was NBA-level good. He went on to become a college All-American, an Olympic champion, and an NBA first-round draft pick. I had no idea he would become brilliant at his craft!

This is where I must talk about my wife. When we met, she was Andrea Carradine. She and her high school friend had come down from the Bay Area (Oakland) to attend California State University Northridge (CSUN). When she arrived as a freshman, I should have already graduated and been on my way with life. However, since I decided to work the modified "7-year graduation plan," I was still in college. I was also one of the student worship leaders for the campus Bible study. When I met her, I could tell she was cool. And though she was a great kid, I had no idea how great she would be as a woman. I had no idea she was brilliant.

In short order, she and her roommate would be Bible study regulars, along with my roommate and some other friends. We became a close-knit group of believers on campus. She was always generous, hospitable, kind, fired up for Jesus Christ, and had a killer cross-over dribble on the basketball court. She could hang with the girls or talk trash with the fellas, and she could quote Scriptures from the Bible with clarity and conviction. She was cute, bright, and had a twinkle in her eye. I was intrigued by her on many levels. The fact that she could ball out on the court and cook in the kitchen was impressive. The fact that she enjoyed watching Magic Johnson and the Showtime Lakers was the icing on the cake. As incredible as she was, she was still five years my junior, which was a large age gap in college. As a result, she didn't register in my mind as a possible romantic interest. At least not yet.

Over the next couple of years, my roommate got involved with a young lady from off campus, and I ended up spending more "alone time" with Andrea. We spent more time together for a variety of unplanned reasons. We became buddies, traveling partners, and the designated "plus 1" on some occasions. One of the turning points (in my mind) was a particular wedding season when some college friends began to get married. Since she had a car and I didn't at the time, she provided transportation to such events. As you know, during wedding season, something is in the air, and everyone looks magically better. I found myself noticing her beauty more and more over time. There was no question that she had great qualities, from her spirituality to her love for sports. But I was still aware of that age gap. I was also aware that sometimes people connect simply because of their proximity to one another. Another complicating factor was that she had a couple of male interests back home in the Bay Area who were interested in a long-term relationship with her. Both had jobs and cars, while I had neither. I knew both fellas as they had come to LA to visit and hang out before. At the time, I was comfortable just being good friends amid our college fellowship. Besides, I was still focused on my seven-year graduation plan!

A Turning Point!

Have you ever had one of those all-night conversations with a friend of the opposite sex where the time just seemed to fly by until the crack of dawn? Well, we had one of those at her house one Friday night, and things took a definite turn. For some reason, I felt so comfortable with her that I felt it was OK to kiss her. It just seemed like the right thing to do, so I did. Now, for context, I was still the "older guy" from Bible Study who led praise and worship and helped run things. She was still very much one of the younger college students in our fellowship. So even though we hung out a lot, I was still the "elder" among us and still the guy who should have graduated already. At that moment, I knew I had a decision to make. Either seriously consider her as more than a friend and a legitimate romantic interest or make an abrupt about-face and never do that again! To be clear, I was not trying to have sex, and neither was she. We both believed that sexual intercourse should be reserved for marriage, according to the Bible. So, avoiding sex was not my primary concern. My concern was that I did not want to lead her to think I wanted an exclusive relationship when I did not.

I learned the hard way what it means to lead someone on. In a previous encounter with a young lady, I inferred that I loved her (as a brother in the Lord), and as a result, she began talking about having kids and making plans to go to David's Bridal. I was totally blindsided! It turned out that her thirst to be loved after a painful relationship experience led her to view my words of affirmation like a payroll check that should be cashed immediately. When I finally was able to clarify that I didn't love her romantically, she did an emotional about-face and cursed the very ground I walked on. I went from being an angel to a devil in a matter of seconds. I vowed NEVER to be that careless with a woman's emotions again. I did not want to put myself in that position with Andrea. I began to fast and pray about what happened, what I wanted, and what this all meant. Could it be that I was falling in love with her? Yes. Could I see myself with her as a romantic interest AND life partner? Yes. I already knew I would eventually be looking for a wife. But was she that person? Yes!

Over the next few days, I began to feel peace about her being a romantic interest. I could see us together for life. And this is where things went off the rails.

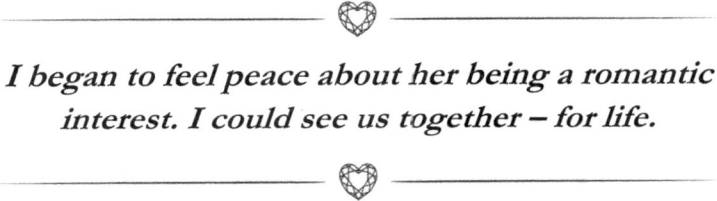

I began to feel peace about her being a romantic interest. I could see us together – for life.

Eighteen Reasons I Should NOT Be Married!

I hadn't really intended to propose marriage but rather to have a discussion with her about the possibilities of a meaningful relationship together. Little did I know that she was already "there" and just waiting for me to catch a clue. She had a sense that we were supposed to be together but never expressed it.

Prior to attempting any "real" proposal, I had planned to let her know that I felt she was "the one" after much consideration and prayer. However, somewhere between catching a clue and sharing my heart with her over a spring semester dinner, I decided to put my fledgling engineering school analytical reasoning to use. That's right, after hearing from God as clearly as I have on any issue in life, I decided to solidify my "findings" by listing all the pros and cons of a life together with Andrea. This was my vain attempt to erase all doubt about any other romantic or relational options.

What could go wrong?

Everything! My attempted exercise to substantiate why we should be married turned into a list of eighteen (yes, eighteen) reasons why we SHOULD NOT be married. It got worse. I had already planned to go on a date with her and share my heart about how I felt and about settling down with "someone" one day. It was supposed to be a step toward togetherness because, at that time, we weren't officially dating or a couple. We were just good friends who were hanging out more and more. But rather than taking a step closer, I helped us take a step away from a viable relationship. She knew what God had spoken to her heart. She could see the "good news" coming a mile away. What she could not see was that the date would not be a reason to celebrate. It turned into my ill-fated attempt at transparency, logical thought, and practical decision-making. Rather than affirming my love and willingness to commit to a long-term relationship, I proceeded to give her eighteen reasons why it would be a bad idea. I am certain that in her mind, they were eighteen sorry excuses.

After hearing the first few reasons, she quickly got the unpleasant picture. I think I may have articulated that our age difference (five years), church background (I was Word of Faith, she was Missionary Baptist), and geographical upbringing (South Central Los Angeles and East Oakland) were reasons that seemingly pointed to incompatibility. For the life of me, I can't recall the other fifteen reasons I dutifully scribed onto green engineering paper. We never got to all eighteen reasons before she abruptly ended the date.

The expression on her face went from expectation and anticipation to confusion and disappointment. That disappointment turned into a resolve to end the date as soon as possible. There was nothing more to say. To make matters more awkward, since we drove in her car, I had little choice but to end it as well. She was devastated. I was confused. The ride home was deadly silent. I was at a loss as to how to make this right, to explain further, to clarify my intentions, and to somehow salvage what appeared to be unsalvageable. The next few days and weeks had me in a fog of confusion. I was not confused about the sudden awkwardness of our once great friendship but confused about how I got "here" in the first place. I knew she was special. I knew she held a unique place in my heart. We had been partners, buddies, and homies for a good minute. I even attempted to help her with her calculus homework, a class in which I had also struggled several times! Among the cute girls in our circle of friends or in our church circle, she stood out from the crowd. I knew she was the "right" one for me. I also knew that I had zero desire to search for someone else.

So, what the heck happened? I am not sure I know to this day. The best spiritual-sounding answer I can come up with for my blunder was something Paul said in **Galatians 1:16** regarding his call from God. To paraphrase, he did not "confer with flesh and blood" to validate something that was revealed to him by the spirit. I attempted to use my limited linear intellect to identify natural reasons why something God spoke to me about or revealed to me was true. Sometimes, as a believer in Christ, you just know when God is speaking to you or wants you to do something. But our minds have a way of either talking us out of it or introducing information that confuses the matter. The result is either a lack of action or the wrong action. Call it overthinking, cold feet, paralysis by analysis, or whatever you like. It happened. But even in our brief and awkward post-eighteen reasons separation, I could not get her out of my mind. She was the one.

A Second Chance at Love!

When I *finally* proposed to her in the spring of 1984, I had great intentions but absolutely no clue. And to make things more interesting, I also had no ring! In my defense, we were both still in college and did not have full-time jobs. Regardless, in today's world of social media driven, professionally produced proposals, I would have been a miserable failure. A total loser. Also, she would have been questioned (on social media) about why she would say "yes" to marrying a man who had no ring to propose with. *How are you engaged without a ring to SHOW that you are engaged?* We are not talking about a big, expensive ring; we are talking about ANY ring!

One evening, after our Monday prayer session was over, Andrea needed to go to the office building where she worked part-time to get some paperwork. Even through the hurt and awkwardness, we were still friends. I offered to accompany her so she wouldn't have to go into an empty office building alone at night. After gathering her things, we walked across the street to a park and began to talk. Again, it was then that I profusely apologized for my embarrassing move and told her that she was the only one I was interested in. She was unwilling to listen to my appeal unless I made myself accountable to someone in our church leadership. She wanted the security of someone else knowing about my decision in case I changed my mind. I agreed, and we called one of the leaders, which eventually led to a meeting with the pastor of the church to make it official, even without a ring.

So, since she knew what God had spoken to her, she said yes.

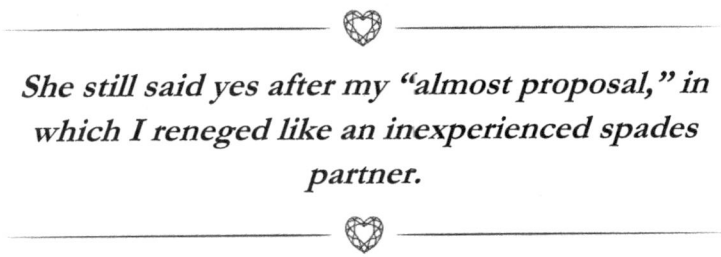

She still said yes after my "almost proposal," in which I reneged like an inexperienced spades partner.

She said yes, even though I was five years older than her. She said yes, when technically, I should have graduated from college before she ever arrived. She said yes when I did not have a full-time job at the time and was still in engineering school. She said yes, even though I was ringless and clueless. Her "yes" despite all the things I did wrong is my constant reminder that God is merciful to fools, babies, and people like me. I was humbled, thankful, and grateful all at once. I don't need any other sign to prove that God loves me!

Despite my less-than-brilliant start and some quirky behavior that could easily look like red flags to others, I was confident we had a solid foundation to build on. Critical elements of our relationship formation were already in place. Even before I get into the Four C's, I firmly believe we had key factors on our side that I don't hear too many couples mention these days. The first one is:

Friendship

We had a strong friendship and genuinely liked being around each other. The fact that we were friends at first played a significant role in how our relationship developed over time. We didn't have the modern "what do you bring to the table?" attitude that really boils down to viewing the other person as either a relationship asset or liability.

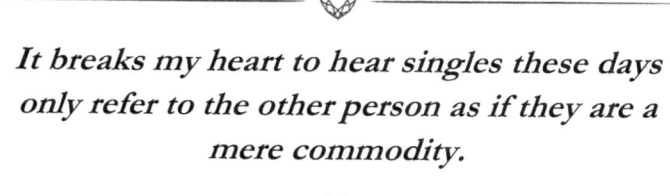

It breaks my heart to hear singles these days only refer to the other person as if they are a mere commodity.

I believe this attitude makes it easier to quit because as soon as they no longer serve your purpose or interest, it's a wrap. Our relationship was not based on social status. We didn't connect because the other person improved our social standing or made us look good in public. To be fair, this was long before the days of posting photos of relationship goals on social media, so that was not a temptation. Our relationship was not based on sexual intimacy. Even after we got together, as Christians, we were both intentional about abstaining from sexual activity. Unfortunately, many couples find their "togetherness" based on sexual contact. And for some men, if their partner does not have sex as a part of the relationship equation, they can easily find another woman who does. The fact that the woman knows he can find sex elsewhere puts pressure on her to engage sexually to keep him. For those who choose to remain sexually pure (as all believers should be), that can present a huge problem! I can hear the wise words of Chaka Khan as she croons, "Once you get started, oh, it's hard to stop," in my ears even now. Sex is one heck of a "bonding agent" in relationships; however, it is not God's glue of choice to keep relationships together long-term. It may not be a popular opinion amongst modern couples, but great friendship provides a better foundation than great sex if a marriage is going to last.

Faith
I am not speaking of a general faith where a person says, I believe there is a God, or I believe in God. I am also not talking about asking God for something and hoping He gives it to you. I am speaking of faith in the thing God specifically revealed to you. I seldom use the "God told me" line. However, if I am sure about anything in my life, it's that I "heard" God when it came to marrying my wife. This wasn't so much an audible voice or words saying, "Thou shalt marry Andrea," but rather a strong inner

sense that God was approving of and confirming our relationship. Even though my "eighteen reasons" debacle nearly derailed us, I ultimately had faith that Andrea was God's choice for me. There was literally no reason to look elsewhere and no other person to pursue. The fact that she stuck around indicates that she had even greater faith that I was God's choice for her. I didn't have to work to convince her of anything because she was already convinced by God.

Don't get me wrong. It's perfectly fine to have a list of preferences, standards, or even non-negotiables in a relationship. Everybody has a list of preferences. But I believe God covers all your preferences (including the ones you don't even know you have) in his choice for you. There is no way I could articulate everything I ever wanted in a wife while I was in college. All I had then was a list based on the here and now. Our "here and now" preferences cannot possibly consider all the ups and downs of life, career changes, relocations, highlights, and hardships. Typically, our greatest fear when trusting God for our partner is thinking He will give us the person we don't want so we can prove that we will obey Him. Guys tend to fear that God will make them marry the ugly girl with great spiritual character. Ladies loathe being stuck with the "nice guy" with zero personality and a low-paying job. Here's the real deal: God knows who is best for you both now and in the future. When He guides you to pick your marriage partner, it will be someone you are attracted to!

God looks at the person who is right for you, not just based on where you are today, but where you are going tomorrow!

Knowing that I had God's choice took the relationship guesswork out of the equation for me. It provided certainty and peace of mind. It meant that I didn't have to look at every potential relationship as a covert interview process. It meant that I didn't have to wonder who really loved me for me or wanted something from me that I could not provide. It meant that I didn't have to keep an eye out for relationship "deal breakers" at every turn. Unlike many couples, we weren't dating to see if we were compatible or if we should get married. We were dating to prepare for marriage.

Chapter Three

Shopping Around

In both my full-time job as a team leader and my other job as a pastor, I have encountered several people who were "shopping." These people were not shopping for bargains at their local department store. They were shopping for answers they wanted to hear. They didn't want to be inconvenienced by unpleasant truths or have to face a harsh reality. Their goal was to seek the answer that they would be comfortable with, even if it wasn't the best answer for them. For example, if an engineer comes to me with a project proposal, I might tell them it will take at least a year for environmental permits to be issued. They may leave my presence to seek a second opinion, only to eventually return to me to file for permits that take a year to be issued. They were shopping for a favorable answer to avoid waiting for the correct process to be completed.

When it comes to marriage, people often have their minds made up before they seek any wisdom, counsel, or advice. Often, they have already determined who they will marry and when. In some cases, I can tell it's the wrong person, for the wrong reason, and at the wrong time in their lives. Just to be clear, I have no interest in telling people not to get married if they really are determined to do so. However, I have no problem telling them my concerns. I tell them that they are not ready and that they should wait a year to address financial issues, destructive habits, or deeply embedded negative mindsets. In these cases, they will often go shopping. They will go to someone else to find the "yes" they want to hear. Sometimes, they return later for counseling to avoid divorce. Most times, they don't return at all because of embarrassment or shame. Nobody wants to hear "I told you so" or to even be confronted with their failure. Their shopping around for a second opinion doesn't change the fact that forming a relationship takes time and energy. Unfortunately, many spend the bulk of their time and energy preparing for a wedding day and not preparing for a married life that will last.

Wait Just a Minute!

Though I wasn't shopping for answers about the right person, I did have to shop for a ring! However, I still had to graduate from college and get a full-time job as an engineer before I could purchase one. Well, a not-so-funny thing happened along the way. Though I was close to a December graduation date, I managed to fail a class that delayed my graduation by a semester. I also conveniently neglected to tell my fiancé about it. In the meantime, we had already begun to make wedding plans for the following summer. Her family was getting involved in the process as well, even to the point of buying wedding gifts they would give to us at Christmas. I didn't have the courage to tell her about the failed class and our potentially shaky financial future.

When we met with our pastor, he noted that we had a sound friendship. But then he observed that we had not been through any testing periods. Little did we know that one was coming sooner than we could possibly imagine! Even though I didn't think I was looking for an "out," I realized that I was looking for a reason to pump the brakes on our plans because of my failure. As soon as the pastor stated that he thought we needed more time, I agreed so quickly that it even surprised me. Though I didn't turn to look at Andrea, I could feel the shock and dismay of a heart betrayed. She was completely blindsided. I had unwittingly delivered an effective emotional gut punch. Everything we discussed up to that point was positive and moving toward marriage. Even our times of prayer and sensing God's presence affirmed that we were on solid footing moving forward. But in a moment, my agreement with the suggestion plunged us into a waiting and testing period that was unexpected. At that moment, I didn't fight for us. At that moment, I didn't fight for her.

This sudden turn of events challenged our relationship greatly. She was angry, hurt, embarrassed, disappointed, and several other things that I didn't want her to feel. She probably felt like she had made a huge mistake. I felt like a complete loser again! I had no idea the devastating impact that my lack of intentionality and indecision would have on our relationship. This ultimately led to six months of her withdrawing the light of her affection and warm spirit from my life. She decided to give me no audience, and I had no words to tell her to change anything. This sent me to a place of prayer and worship to discover who God was in this relationship. It sent us both to a place of seeking. Even in this space, I never doubted that we SHOULD be together, but I wondered if we WOULD be together. Thankfully, in time, I got enough of a glimmer of hope to affirm that she still believed in us – in spite of me!

You Better Shop Around!

Years later, after eventually graduating in the spring of 1986, I secured a full-time job with benefits at the State of California in the fall of the same year. I saved up enough money to buy a ring with cash, and since I worked in downtown Los Angeles, I was able to go to the jewelry district to shop for a ring. The good news was that there was a wide variety of jewelry stores and ring designs to choose from. The bad news was that it was overwhelming to have so many choices. I found myself grappling with questions: *Where do I start? Who do I trust? How much should I spend?* Despite having the funds, I realized I had some decisions to make.

The Four C's for Diamonds

I had no idea what a good diamond was, so I began my haphazard search for the elusive "perfect" ring that would also fit my budget. After seeing lots of diamonds, asking lots of questions, and being offered lots of "unbelievable" deals, I was getting weary of the process. One store merchant mercifully gave me a pamphlet that explained that there are four C's for diamonds. In a nutshell, I discovered that a quality diamond is largely identified by four key characteristics. They are:

- Carat
- Color
- Clarity
- Cut

At least, this initial knowledge provided a foundation for evaluating a diamond. Still, navigating the overwhelming array of jewelry stores in Downtown LA remained a daunting challenge. It was a modest beginning in my quest for the perfect ring!

Allow me to briefly elaborate on the essential characteristics of a gemstone and how they influence its value. We'll delve into similar traits that define the value of a marriage later on.

Carat

Carat is the measure of the weight of diamonds and gemstones. It is the attribute that can have the most profound effect on the value of a diamond because larger (and thereby heavier) diamonds are rarer than smaller ones. If you can find a large diamond (say, three or more carats), it's an extraordinary find. So, when it comes to diamonds, size does matter!

Color

Color refers to the degree to which a diamond is without color or colorless. In fact, the best "color" is no color at all. This allows the greatest amount of pure white light to be reflected through the facets of a diamond so that it sparkles as brightly as possible.

Clarity

Clarity refers to the presence of inclusions in a diamond. Almost all diamonds contain tiny, naturally occurring defects, or "birthmarks," known as inclusions. They also have surface irregularities known as blemishes. These naturally occurring defects also serve to prevent the maximum amount of light from reflecting through a diamond. Fewer inclusions, along with less color, give rise to the greatest amount of brilliance, or "fire," in a diamond. This greatly increases its value.

Cut

Cut refers to the angles and proportions of a diamond. It is the only one of the 4Cs that is crafted by the human hand. It is also deemed the most important characteristic of the 4Cs. The cut is responsible for the diamond's brilliance. A symmetrical, proportionate diamond cut will bring the most sparkle. It is sometimes confused with shape (round, pear, or marquise), but it actually relates to how the facets or plane surfaces are cut. A skilled craftsman will cut a diamond in such a way as to maximize the amount of light reflected from one facet to another, thereby increasing its brilliance or "fire," which leads to greater value. In this one area, man (the craftsman) holds the key to determining a diamond's ascribed value.

Who Sets the Standard?

The 4Cs classification is the framework that enables the comparison and valuation of diamonds. It is the framework established by the Gemological Institute of America (GIA), which is the scientific authority on gems. It is an independent, nonprofit organization that conducts gem research and sets the standards for determining diamond quality. The GIA is not only a unique source for diamond knowledge, but its grading reports also inspire confidence in consumers. These consumers, including museums and private collectors, recognize the importance of complete, unbiased, scientific information in gem assessment and absolutely trust the GIA to provide it.

As you can see, each of the 4Cs above is critical to the overall value of a diamond. For example, a large diamond with a hint of yellow color and numerous inclusions will be reduced in value. A very clear and colorless stone that is poorly cut will not reflect the maximum amount of light and lose value. A smaller diamond with incredible clarity and cut will be more valuable than a large diamond with visible inclusions.

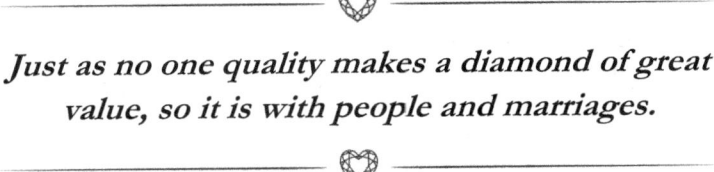

Just as no one quality makes a diamond of great value, so it is with people and marriages.

I believe God Himself acts as the "Spiritual GIA" that independently sets the standard for relationship success and marriage. His purpose and intention for every person and marriage relationship are comprised of a unique, winning combination of attributes that make a marriage both valuable and visually brilliant! By contrast, let's take a moment to discuss some of the faulty standards that present a challenge to marriage brilliance.

Your "Perfect Partner" Shopping List

When I hear about people's criteria for selecting a potential mate (aka "the list"), I usually get concerned. It sometimes reminds me of my search for a diamond ring. I had no real understanding of what really made them valuable or brilliant. Without knowledge of the 4Cs standard, I could have been easily persuaded to buy the biggest stone because bigger is supposed to be better. In the same way, people have long lists of characteristics for the "perfect" person to be in a relationship with. Our initial attraction (by God's design) is largely based on the person with the most visible sparkle. For guys, that "sparkle" is mostly in the form of sexual attraction. She doesn't have to be Miss America, but looking good and making him look good is huge! For girls who want a "good man" to marry, that "sparkle" is often in the form of financial security. He doesn't have to be rich, but it sure helps! Since we are all selfish by nature, we usually gravitate toward the people we think will make us look good or make our lives convenient. The problem is that we often fail to identify the key features that will lead us to experience true marriage brilliance.

Guys typically want a woman who is physically attractive, supportive, believes in him, doesn't give him grief (not argumentative or combative), can cook and clean, and also works out to stay in shape. That "workout" requirement is his way of saying he doesn't want a fat wife. Or at least he doesn't want to have to motivate her to stay in shape or keep herself physically together, especially after having children. He figures if she looks good, he looks good too. I am not mad at those requirements, but these are mostly outward characteristics that don't address marriage dynamics.

What about the ladies?

Ladies tend to want a little more than a man would. They want a man who is tall (at least taller than them), handsome, humorous, sensitive, strong, driven, worldly wise, resourceful, loves kids, and has a job making at least six figures. The six-figure job requirement is her way of saying she doesn't want to be broke or destined to struggle financially. And although she may be willing to support a man while he climbs the corporate ladder, she does not want to carry the relationship financially.

I once heard a comedian joke about the difference between what men and women look for in a relationship. A man will pursue the pretty girl who is working the fries at the local fast-food restaurant. Why? Because she is pretty. End of story! On the other hand, a woman would never pursue a cute guy who is working the fries at a fast-food restaurant. Why not? Because he is working on the fries at a fast-food restaurant! Working there may be good for a kid in high school or working his way through college, but it is not a picture of a successful man who can support a woman who wants to get married and raise a family. The reasoning behind the difference is simple. The man wants the pretty. The woman wants the provider.

Part II:
Facets

Every diamond has facets.

A facet is defined as "one side of something many-sided, especially of a cut gem." In our context, it refers to any flat, polished surface on a diamond or other gemstone. The purpose of the facets on the pavilion of a diamond is to redirect light. After the light has entered, it is refracted back through the crown as flashes of light. The standard round-cut gem has 58 facets or sides. Some diamond shapes may have up to 144 facets. Though the number of facets of a diamond may vary with style, an ideal or excellent cut diamond is well-proportioned with optimal facet angles.

Similarly, every person has facets. No person is all one thing or described by a single character trait, gift, strength, or personality type.

There are an incredible number of tests and assessments that are designed to help people identify and maximize their personalities and perspectives. Some common assessments used by employers are Myers Briggs, DISC, and Strengths Finder.

These allow employers to more easily identify personality traits in individuals who may work for their companies. Even with these sophisticated tests, they do not reveal all the facets of a person. In fact, even among people who "score" in the same category, their individual facets will differentiate them from one another. We all reflect the same light (information) to different degrees and in different ways. God has uniquely crafted us with the optimal number of facets and facet angles for His purpose to be fulfilled on earth. Hopefully, throughout your life, you will have discovered and embraced many of your facets. Then, you can be sure that as you enter marriage, you will discover many more of your facets as well as those of your partner. Let's go!

Chapter Four

Facets, Flaws, and Faux Cs

Just like a diamond, every individual is multi-faceted. That's how we were crafted by God. Within the comparatively crude categories identified by personality assessments, there are layers and levels to each of our lives. Some facets are passed down through our DNA, and some are acquired from our environment or experiences. The traits we consider to be strengths in our lives are also coupled with corresponding weaknesses or flaws, as with diamonds.

The flaws or defects in a diamond are commonly referred to as "inclusions." No natural diamond is completely flawless, even though some are advertised as such based on how they are viewed under a 10x microscope. In some cases, flaws are microscopic. On the other hand, sometimes external or internal flaws can be observed with the naked eye. External flaws or blemishes like scratches, nicks, and chips are found on the surface. Internal flaws or inclusions, like pinpoints and crystals, are inside the diamond. Sometimes, a diamond appears to be cloudy, and other times, you can see a dot or speck of black carbon inside the diamond. These blemishes and inclusions can influence the brilliance and, as a result, the overall value of the diamond. However, it is still a diamond. Based on the buyer's budget, the diamond will still be purchased despite the presence of minor or microscopic flaws.

Can I stop right here to tell you that the person that you plan to marry or have married will have multiple facets that enhance their brilliance? Those are the things that likely attracted you to them. But they will also have flaws—blemishes and inclusions—that can potentially diminish their brilliance. But unlike the permanence of a diamond, human flaws present an opportunity. Our mistakes are often an opportunity for God to demonstrate the life-changing power of his glorious light in the marriage experience!

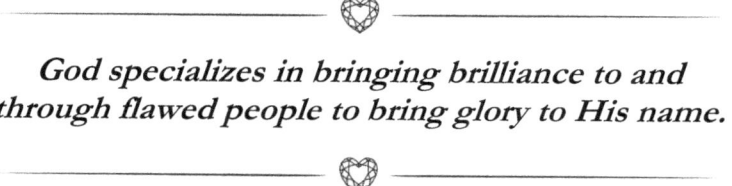

God specializes in bringing brilliance to and through flawed people to bring glory to His name.

While you may be looking for or wishing you had a flawless partner, please know that God is not limited to using or redeeming "perfect" people. In fact, he specializes in bringing brilliance to and through flawed people to bring glory to His name. I am certain that every married couple begins to discover surprising new facets and flaws about their partner as soon as the words "I do" spill from their lips. Sometimes, the honeymoon exposes new facets and flaws that may have been overlooked earlier. For those who did not cohabitate before marriage, the first night alone together can be shocking, inspiring, or both! And, of course, times of crisis reveal facets and flaws that even you and your partner didn't realize existed. My point is that all of us are multi-faceted individuals, more so than we even know. All of us have flaws that we either try to hide or never knew existed. Each of those facets and flaws presents an opportunity for the marriage to shine and express the brilliance of God in some way.

Faux Cs in a Marriage

Many of the external characteristics we often focus on, such as good looks (for a woman) and material wealth (for a man), may be factors that lead to a couple getting married. However, they are often not foundational for enduring marriage brilliance or long-term resilience. So, when marriages and long-term relationships fall apart, we sometimes make the following comments:

But they were so **cute** together.
They seemed to have such great **chemistry.**
She was so **charming.**
He was so **charismatic.**

And if you are a Christian, you may have made comments like this:

But they were both raised in the **church**.

They were both good **Christian** people.

They were both **called** to an incredible ministry.

I hope you appreciate the fact that I worked hard to make sure that the words I highlighted all begin with the letter C. But they are not the "Cs" that lead to a brilliant marriage! I call them "faux" or fake Cs because they can appear to lead to relationship success. Again, these characteristics are not bad in and of themselves. But when placed under the microscope of a marriage relationship, these characteristics don't hold up as well as we think they should. Let me explain why these characteristics, though often glorified, make my Faux Cs list below.

Cute Together

Stop me if you have ever read this on a tabloid before:

Shocking News: A Hollywood couple files for divorce!

Yeah, this "shocking news" is often some of the most predictable news we will ever see. In fact, we universally have a low expectation that great-looking celebrity couples will ever have a lengthy marriage. They may be deemed the "pretty people," cute together, or voted the "sexiest couple" of the year. Unfortunately, that doesn't translate into longevity or happiness. Kim Kardashian and professional basketball player Kris Humphries divorced after 72 days, citing irreconcilable differences (surprise). Pop music superstars Usher and Grace Miguel lasted 2.5 years. Comedian Russell Brand and singer Katy Perry hung in there for 14 months. Songstress Mariah Carey and actor and TV personality Nick Cannon divorced after six years. The list goes on.

Even though reality show relationships may seem glamorous, they are not without their challenges. The constant pressure to perform, maintain a perfect public image, travel incessantly, keep up with insane work schedules, and remain relevant to the public can put a strain on any marriage. Good looks and Hollywood success can lead to physical attraction, social media fame, and red-carpet accolades. But the good looks or the look of success alone may not be enough to land you a role in a blockbuster marriage!

Charismatic

Charisma is defined as "compelling attractiveness or charm that can inspire devotion in others." It can also be described as an individual's ability to attract and influence other people. This is a great skill or gift that, when displayed on a first date or early in the dating process, can certainly be exciting to experience. It is a great quality in a relationship only if it is displayed within the confines of the relationship. Let me explain. Some people display their charisma best before an audience, on stage, or in public spaces. This gets them noticed, celebrated, and even paid, which is a good thing! Charisma can help a person win friends and influence other people. There is an incentive to "turn on the charm" during a networking event or on the red carpet moments of life. Unfortunately, far too often, the "charm" is turned off when we get home. The charm can also wear off under the stress of a marriage if that is not truly how a person shows up in life.

I am not here to bash charisma or charm. It's an incredible gift. But it can also be used to cover up glaring areas of weakness in a relationship. I have seen how the same person who gets raving reviews from co-workers and adoring fans does not get the same response from their spouse. Sometimes, it's because a person has adapted their behavior to shine in the big "on stage" moments. When the moment is over, there is no reason to shine. Assuming someone will be charismatic in every life situation is like assuming a comedian will have you in stitches both on stage and at home.

Famed comedian Robin Williams made millions laugh with his genius wit, but he was not able to overcome the mental and emotional health issues he faced. It is documented that he had a long history of both addiction and depression. My only warning to those who may be tempted to be drawn into a relationship with an extremely charismatic person is this: observe them in a variety of scenarios and over time. When do they turn charisma on, and when do they turn it off? Is it only activated for those outside close family relationships or for those inside as well? Is it demonstrated only to those from whom they might benefit? Is it also demonstrated to people who can't do anything for them? Be honest with yourself about who they really are in every situation of life to gauge how their gift might translate to your relationship.

Chemistry

Even though I barely passed my chemistry classes in college, I did learn some important principles.

First, I understood that for a chemical reaction to take place, you need at least two different reactants to make a specific product. Secondly, the reactants must be combined in proper proportions to get the right product. For example, common table salt is composed of two dangerous elements: sodium (a highly reactive metal) and chlorine (a reactive yellow-green gas). Individually, each element can be dangerous in certain conditions. But when their atoms are combined in proper proportions, salt is indispensable to our daily lives. Sodium (Na) and chlorine (Cl) combine in a 1:1 ratio (1 sodium atom + 1 chlorine atom) to make a salt molecule. You can't randomly substitute any other element and expect to get salt. Also, excess amounts of any single element will leave those atoms in an unreacted state, which is still potentially dangerous. When excess chlorine is unable to react because all the sodium molecules are used up, that leaves unreacted chlorine on the table. Excess chlorine will create a poisonous atmosphere, while excess sodium can create an explosive environment!

What in the world does this have to do with marriages? I am so glad you asked. First, chemistry is an amazing thing in relationships. It is most often tied to romance, but great chemistry can also be experienced between co-workers on project teams and in other collaborative relationships. Great chemistry can happen in movie or music production as well as in any business enterprise where people are on the same page. It goes beyond just wanting to create a great product or run a successful business. It's a deeper connection, respect, and understanding.

In marriage, however, I think chemistry should be considered a miracle of God. That's because it's not just two simple "elements" coming together to predictably form a molecule. It is two extremely diverse, complex, and nuanced "compounds" or people connecting to accomplish a specific goal. In marriage, the two different individuals intentionally "react" with one another to create something good, positive, and, yes, even brilliant. So, when people say, "We have great chemistry," they are usually referring to how the other person makes them feel, how they connect or "vibe," and even how they experience a tangible "electricity" or magic when they are together.

Being Extra

This is where I want to introduce the concept of being "extra" in a relationship. Great chemistry in relationships happens when both parties (elements) bring just the right amount of themselves together. That could be any combination of their strengths and weaknesses, passions, and personality traits. But what if things change over time? What if the person who brings great emotional energy into a relationship begins to bring "extra" emotional energy in the form of worry, fear, or anxiety? That "extra" emotional energy will throw off the chemistry and the expected reaction. Just like with chemical elements, that "extra" wants to go somewhere to react with something.

A partner who excels at managing all the relationship details can be an invaluable asset when they do so in the right measure. But when that attention to detail becomes "extra" and turns into micromanagement or control, it becomes a problem. Also, a partner who likes to take risks can be great for having exciting new experiences. But when that partner takes "extra" risks without regard to their relationship's health, they can become a burden. A partner who has a teaching gift, when in excess, can come across as constantly correcting or even scolding. The very thing that drove you to connection, when in excess, can easily become the thing that drives you crazy!

Having that spark, energy, excitement, and connection creates amazing brilliance in a relationship. It can be fuel, encouragement, and confirmation that you are with the right person. It can be especially visible during the honeymoon or in the early stages of a relationship. However, when chemistry begins to wane or is out of balance, sometimes people believe it is a signal that the marriage might be over.

All Chemistry Ain't Good Chemistry!

The reason I don't want to elevate chemistry in a relationship to lofty status is that it sometimes depends on how people connect at different times in their lives. If you ever read accounts of people (male or female) who have had an affair or cheated on their spouse, you might hear how they first lost chemistry or connection. Not coincidentally, at the same time, they may have met someone who finally "gets them" or whom they connect with more than their spouse. For men, this could be with the divorced soccer mom on the sidelines at his kids' soccer games whom he feels free to share his feelings with. Her sympathy and attention may create a connection that he hasn't felt from his wife in years. For women, it could be the younger, energetic male coworker who expresses concern about her marriage challenges. His level of sensitivity and understanding seem like a true gift. The ways in which he demonstrates care and honor for her are intriguing.

The excitement of just having someone see you and care about you is stimulating and can be a welcomed relief from the marriage routine. The idea of a new relationship or love interest can often prove intoxicating. When the negatives of the current relationship are contrasted with the allure and excitement of a potential relationship, it can create the perfect setup for an affair. This, too, is chemistry.

The elements of marriage detachment, disengagement, and disconnection combined with attention, acceptance, and affirmation often create a potent mixture leading to unfaithfulness. The good news is that, with some effort, the process is reversible, and new chemistry can be developed when couples are intentional about discovering new connections within their relationship. So yes, chemistry is an extremely important and desirable element of a relationship. I just believe that we must be careful not to make it the leading indicator of relationship success or failure.

Church Affiliation

You may have heard the saying that goes, "Just because you park yourself in the garage, that doesn't make you a car!" Experience has shown us that just because a person goes to church, that doesn't make them a Christian. We all know people who either go to church or say they were raised in the church. That is not a bad thing. The bad thing is when their values and actions don't reflect "church" or, more importantly, Jesus Christ! When very little of what Christ teaches is reflected in their personal lives, there are bound to be problems in relationships.

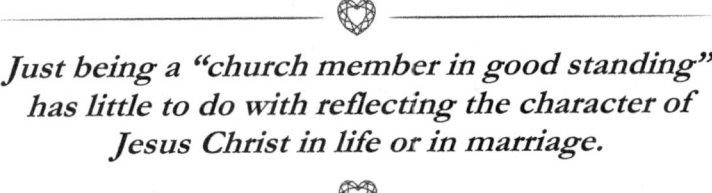

Just being a "church member in good standing" has little to do with reflecting the character of Jesus Christ in life or in marriage.

As a pastor, I love to see people flourish in a healthy church environment. The church is a God-designed space for people to become familiar with biblical values and develop a thriving relationship with God. But if we are honest with ourselves, that doesn't always happen. There are myriad reasons why, and we can't cover them all here. But in some cases, the church environment is just plain unhealthy. People are sometimes prone to come away from a church with bad theology, bad habits, and bad experiences. In other cases, the individual attended church for cosmetic reasons. Some people are totally fine with being considered Christian in name only for social reasons, even if it is not practiced in their lives. Our Western church culture has historically implied that church attendance equates to being a good, religious, or moral person. Nothing could be further from the truth.

Let me provide a few case studies that illustrate my point:

1. Church Girl

I know a young man who got married while he served in a branch of the military. He married a "church girl," whom he figured was a safe bet to match the faith he found in college. They met in a local church near where he was stationed and were married in that same church. Several months after they were married, he was deployed.

Upon his return, he found that, in addition to being a church girl, she was quite the party girl. Stepping out on the town and spending his money quickly became a habit she didn't want to give up. It seemed that once she "escaped" her traditional church confines and parents into a married life, she decided to let her hair down – all the way down! It seemed as if he returned from his deployment to a completely different wife. From all appearances, she had been deprived in the church environment and was finally free. As a result of her "wilding out" behavior, he eventually set her free for good through divorce. I know her case is not unique. So, let's stop acting surprised when someone who was raised in the church, regularly attends church, or got married in the church has a failed relationship. Being in church doesn't change a person's behavior any more than being parked in a garage can turn an everyday garden tool into a sports car.

2. Covert and Codependent

During our college years, my soon-to-be wife and I had a friend who got married while she, too, was still in college. The guy she was going to marry was already working a full-time job. They were both Christian people who regularly attended church. At some point, they moved from Los Angeles to northern California, in the vicinity of her family and church. We had a chance to visit them and their toddler during the Christmas holidays one year. In addition to the joy of reconnecting with our friends, we were heartbroken to hear how they had financial challenges because he was robbed of his entire paycheck at gunpoint. Fortunately, they were able to get some financial help from her family. We promised to keep them in prayer as we traveled back to Los Angeles. Later, we found out he had mysteriously "lost" or had been robbed of other paychecks during their brief time being married. We were completely unprepared for the reality of what was going on. It turns out that he had a severe drug addiction and was literally "blowing" the rent money on drugs. This "Christian" marriage failed soon thereafter due to the stress placed on it by lies, deception, and drug addiction. Clearly, it would have taken a ton of work to salvage, let alone maintain this relationship. But in that instant, our naivete about "Christian marriages" was dealt a debilitating blow.

3. Churchy and Charging It!

An older couple got married as both parties were seeking a fresh start in love after previous failed relationships. The man was relatively new to his faith but sincere. The woman, from all appearances, had been in church her entire life. They met during a season when they were both serving in a community service organization. They were beyond the age of having children, and his youngest was already in college. So, raising kids or trying to manage a blended family was not an issue. Supporting kids financially wasn't a major concern aside from helping the college-aged child with rent from time to time. After being married for a few years, he soon discovered that she had developed the bad habit of secretly establishing charge accounts at major department store chains across the country. For reference, this was back in the days when you walked into a bank with your paycheck on a Friday afternoon to make your deposit. You were not notified immediately about transactions or accounts linked to your name. There was no technology to send you a text message alert about any suspicious account activity. Apparently, she felt that she had hit the jackpot to the point where she was willing to share his good credit status with her family in other parts of the United States. When they got divorced, he was left to untangle a web of credit card debt, not to mention the spiritual and emotional impacts of being betrayed by a good "churchy" Christian woman in the process.

4. Called to Ministry

Another young couple we knew got married and relocated to a different state because he was called to ministry as a youth pastor. She was a pastor's daughter who demonstrated a great deal of spiritual maturity and wisdom. He was the leader of a gospel music group and an engaging young preacher. We were excited to see this promising young couple launch out to serve God. After visiting them on a couple of occasions; we overlooked some relationship red flags. I recall us believing a story about how a bedroom door had somehow developed a hole in it. At the time, it was explained away as a household accident. Later, it was revealed that they were covering up the evidence of a heated argument where the husband punched a hole in the door. The reason the door had a hole in it was because his fist just barely missed his young wife's head.

The promising young minister was confronted more than once for having inappropriate relationships with multiple young women in the ministry where he served. In a short time, a multi-layered cake built on lies, broken promises, confrontations, and denials was also sprinkled with financial mismanagement. Ultimately, it led to a divorce, and she moved back to California. He was dismissed from his pastoral duties. Both his promising marriage and ministry were undermined by his lack of self-control when it came to the opposite sex, among other things. He was a great minister to the masses but hardly a great marriage partner.

Please don't misunderstand my point. By sharing these cases, I am in no way attempting to bash Christian marriages or minimize the value of a faith-based relationship. In the same way that I believe marriage is God's institution, I also believe that two people who intend to honor God in their marriage relationship are positioned for marital success. Therein lies the rub. Two people must be intentional about honoring God in their marriage. Those who both believe in the life-transforming power of God's Word and His Holy Spirit are equipped with spiritual resources designed to assist them in marriage and in life. It doesn't make a Christian marriage better than a non-Christian marriage; it just potentially provides different tools for the parties involved. But those resources can only impact a relationship if they are properly utilized and put into action. I want to stress again that all of us have both facets and flaws that influence our behavior, decisions, and experiences. All of us have blind spots and bad days. The fact that a person is a believer in Jesus doesn't make their flaws magically disappear. Faith in God doesn't eliminate bad days.

We might be inclined to assume that an individual or couple called to ministry is more spiritually mature than the average couple. We presume that their calling in one area qualifies them to be astute in another. A person or persons who are called by God to minister or lead others may have specific gifts or skills for that calling. They should also have developed a certain level of godly character in their lives. We don't expect them to be liars, cheaters, sexually loose, or generally immoral. Rather, we expect them to act spiritually mature! What does that look like in real life? It looks like people who are operating with specific characteristics the Bible refers to as the "fruit of the spirit," according to **Galatians 5:22-23,**

> *"But the fruit of the Spirit is love, joy, peace, longsuffering, kindness, goodness, faithfulness, gentleness, and self-control. Against such, there is no law.*
> *And those who are Christ's have crucified the flesh with its passions and desires.*
> *If we live in the Spirit, let us also walk in the Spirit.*
> *Let us not become conceited, provoking one another, envying one another."*

Without launching into a sermon on the fruit of the Spirit, if we just use these verses as a personal behavior checklist in our marriages, we will likely see success. If we are bringing love, joy, and peace to our partners, they will certainly have less to complain about. If we were long-suffering and kind, that would eliminate a lot of friction. Practicing goodness, faithfulness, and self-control would keep tempers from flaring. These qualities function completely independent of cuteness, charisma, chemistry, or compatibility. These are distinct from personal gifting, talent, or anointing. These qualities need to be developed. So, when it comes to a calling to minister to the masses, there is no guarantee that these traits will be part of the package.

In fact, it may have nothing to do with how a person operates in their marriage. Sometimes, the "calling" to ministry reveals and exposes the weaknesses in a person's character and in the marriage. At other times, ministry itself can be the source of marriage friction, frustration, or failure. In some cases, individuals have grappled with the question of what should be the ultimate priority in pleasing God: the marriage or ministry? When both parties in a marriage relationship have different views on this subject, things can get tense!

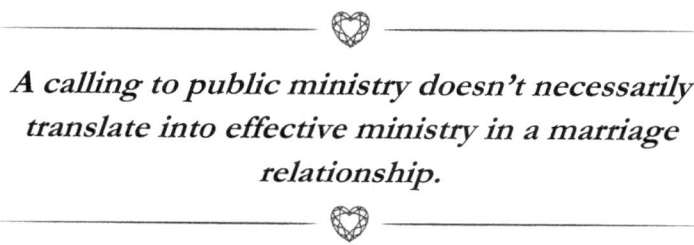

A calling to public ministry doesn't necessarily translate into effective ministry in a marriage relationship.

Conflicted Callings?

So, does God make mistakes when calling some people to both marriage and ministry? Does one have a higher value than the other? Should they both be balanced like weights on the scales of justice or should one concede precedence to the other? To be honest, I don't see a lot of Old Testament prophets and priests having the perfect "balance" of ministry office hours, family vacation time, and attending kids' soccer games. I can't think of any New Testament Bible leaders rushing to make it to the kids' dance recital or helping the wife start a small business. This may be because the Bible largely documents the lives of prophets, kings, and leaders who had national prominence and influence in

Jewish culture. Their family life was often not in the spotlight; their obedience to God was.

That's what we see with so many Old and New Testament leaders – the specific work they were called to do. They were called to speak God's Word with boldness, stand resolutely against wickedness, call out unrighteousness, institute reforms, pray for revival, and even conquer enemy nations. Those callings were their life's work and purpose on earth. It's not that some didn't have other occupations or marriage relationships. Those other things are just not highlighted in Scripture.

Now, let's take a look at those "spiritual tasks" in the context of marriage. Nothing about conquering nations speaks to loving your wife or submitting to your husband. Nothing about ministering to the multitudes addresses who should wash the dishes or do the laundry. There is not much mention of who is most fiscally responsible or who can cook the best tuna casserole. Let's stop equating a person's calling to ministry with their ability to operate in a successful marriage relationship. I think it's unrealistic to expect a person who has devoted their life to ministering to masses of people (a grace and a developed skill) to automatically know how to minister to a spouse. That, too, is a developed skill. That said, I am certainly not giving a pass to ministers for being negligent husbands or wives because of the high calling of God on their lives. It's not an either-or proposition. It's a BOTH–AND proposition. God may have called you into ministry, but you made a vow before the same God in marriage. So, if you are going to do both ministry and marriage, then do both as unto the Lord.

To my anointed and appointed brother, preacher, pastor, minister, apostle, or whoever you are, you cannot pull out the "she needs to get with the vision" or "she knew who she was marrying" card to justify neglecting your marital responsibilities. She is not just married to you; you are also married to her by your own choice.

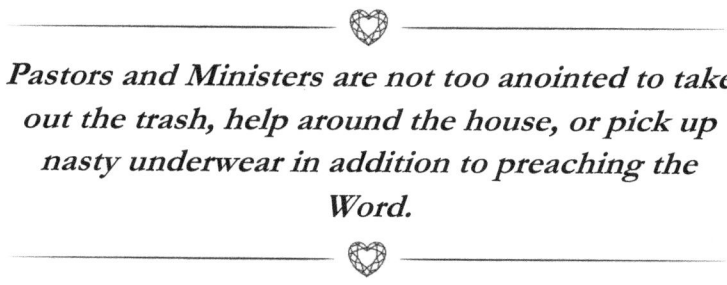

Pastors and Ministers are not too anointed to take out the trash, help around the house, or pick up nasty underwear in addition to preaching the Word.

For my sisters who are called to be blazing hot, on-fire evangelists, teachers, prayer warriors, and intercessors, it's both marriage and ministry. Remember, even if your husband possesses different "spiritual gifts," he should never be treated as a lower priority in God's kingdom. He is not merely married to you; you made a sacred vow to honor him before the Lord.

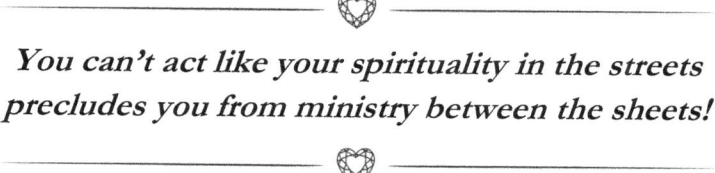

You can't act like your spirituality in the streets precludes you from ministry between the sheets!

God wants to be glorified in both the ministry that he called you to and the marriage you vowed to be faithful in because He ordained both! If it means acquiring vastly different skillsets to be effective in both, then it's time to level up in one area or another for His glory!

Maintaining the Garden

At the risk of sounding sacrilegious, I want to challenge the idea that a "Christian marriage" (whatever we think that is) should automatically be a successful marriage. Now, please don't get me wrong; I am a firm believer that individuals who have given their lives to Christ should prayerfully seek His direction on life decisions, including whom to marry. Additionally, I believe that God can and does want to direct our paths to the "right" person. He wants to bless, prosper, and sustain the marriage union that He brought together! But all those steps I discussed only represent the beginning. Seeking God and finding His choice for marriage is the equivalent of graduating from college and getting your first job. Yes, you and your loved ones should celebrate this huge milestone! But you still have a whole career and life ahead of you. So, in one sense, yes, you have arrived. But in another sense, you have only just begun. Now is the time to get to work!

We are quick to say things like, "*If God ordained it, He will sustain it.*" These and other catchy phrases may sound good on a Sunday morning. They may even sound great in a social media post. But this is only partly true. This is where we should take a lesson from Adam. God certainly **ordained** Adam to be in the garden. God certainly **sustained** Adam in the garden by providing abundant food resources. But God gave Adam the responsibility (translation: *a job*) to **maintain** the garden. Being ordained to be married and sustained by God's provision in marriage is just part of the picture. There are some things each Christian person in the relationship must do to maintain the relationship. It's that dreaded four-letter word called Work. By work, I am not just talking about the man going out to work in a factory or an office while the woman is managing the home or taking the kids to soccer practice. There may be variations on those traditional roles depending on the dynamics of life. The work involved in maintaining the garden of your marriage may look different in every relationship and for every individual, but it must be done. In many cases, the most difficult work is not doing everyday tasks and household responsibilities. The "work" may include addressing unreasonable expectations, negative mindsets, or destructive habits! If we are unwilling to do the work, we can be Christians in name only and not experience the fullness of the glorious provisions we have in Christ. If we are unwilling to do the work, we can also be married in name only and not experience the fullness of God's provision for our marriage.

The Garden was ordained and sustained by God but was maintained by Adam. He had to do the work.

Love is Not Enough

Most people think love will enable marriages to overcome anything. That's what romantic movies tell us, but I wholeheartedly disagree.

Don't get me wrong. I am not anti-love, and I don't think love is insignificant. The feeling of emotional love creates an attraction that brings two people together. The decision to love beyond feelings and emotions is an indispensable component of any relationship. But people fall in love every day and express their love in a variety of ways. Often, those expressions of love (and their limitations) are based on their upbringing, experiences, and who modeled love for them. That love may also be founded in what they have been fed by television, movies, culture, and society.

Just consider for a moment the little girl who has been fed a steady diet of Disney princesses and their respective Prince Charming. Her idea of love is likely based on the excitement of having Prince Charming sweep her off her feet. Those stories conveniently end with, "And they lived happily ever after," even though nobody sees the "ever after" part! Contrast that with the little boy who saw his father provide financially for his family while being emotionally detached or even abusive towards his wife and kids. His view of love may be limited to providing for material needs. The absence of emotional expression informs him that love looks like putting a roof over the family's head and food on the table. These are both gross oversimplifications, but my point is that neither is based on a healthy reality. Both have been set up to expect different things from this thing called love.

Whenever unhealthy expectations are expressed in marriage, the feelings of love can dissipate as quickly as a summer rain in the Florida heat. In one hour, it may be coming down in sheets, but in the next, you can see the steam evaporating from the hot pavement. If love is based on emotional or erotic feelings, you can be sure it's going to change over time.

In many cases, it's not the absence of love but rather the presence of unhealthy expectations or destructive behaviors that separate couples.

Like an invasive plant species, multiple habits and hang-ups can be far too much for "love" to overcome. Moreover, contrary to the popular adage, love does NOT conquer all, especially when it is greatly outnumbered! Over time, the number of "enemies" to your love and marital bliss can seem to multiply to insurmountable proportions, like zombies in a cheap horror movie. We could literally go through the alphabet and name the internal and external factors that erode or ruin marriage relationships: *absence, abuse, boredom, comparison, drama, distrust, disappointment, disloyalty, drug addiction, extramarital affairs, fear, fantasy, grudges, hatred, indifference, infidelity, inconsistency, jealousy, kleptomania, loneliness, materialism, mental instability, narcissism, negativity, obsessing,*

pornography, quarreling, resistance, selfishness, stubbornness, tedium, uncertainty, vanity, weak-willed, xenophobia, yelling, and *zealotry.*

Here is a home exercise for you:

Take some time to interview a few people you know who are separated or divorced. Ask them what led to their separation or divorce. Even if they totally blame the other person and excuse themselves, you will gather important data to compile a list of what their love was up against. Even interview those who survived the nastiest of divorces and ask them to identify the issues that created a wedge between them. You may be surprised at the number and variety of "enemies" that successfully overran their love. It wasn't that they never loved or fell in love with the other person. Unfortunately, in many cases, they "fell out of love" or discovered they had "irreconcilable differences" that their love could not overcome.

Love Needs Some Backup!

As much as love is a necessary ingredient in any relationship, it can't do the job of maintaining a relationship alone. It needs assistance. It needs help. It needs support. In relationships, love needs backup, the same way a mall cop needs backup during a Black Friday brawl. He may be legally authorized to maintain a certain level of order and discourage larceny through his very presence. However, his flashlight and badge won't help much in a crowd of hostile shoppers. He needs law enforcement backup. Building on the law enforcement theme, we tend to think that love is like the sheriff in a Western who keeps the relationship "town" civil and orderly. So, we say things like, "If you really love me, you will do _____ (fill in the blank)." Or we ask, "How can you say you love me if you keep doing XYZ?" The behavior may not reflect a lack of love. It may reflect a greater lack of maturity, self-control, or commitment. It may reflect past trauma or co-dependency. It may be the result of a deep-seated fear or insecurity that overshadows the person's capacity to love. So, in the case of our "love sheriff," no matter how skilled he is with a six-shooter, he needs the support and cooperation of decent, law-abiding citizens. When those law-abiding citizens outnumber the few potentially unruly characters, things in the town usually go well. They, along with the sheriff, create a culture of lawfulness in the town. The characters that would otherwise conduct themselves unlawfully know their desire to "act out" will not be tolerated by the good town folk.

When it comes to our relationships, we think that love can single-handedly outgun every bad guy who "acts out" to disrupt the relationship's "town" of peace and harmony. Love needs the support of law-abiding citizens like common sense, compassion, courage, and courtesy to maintain a culture of civility in the relationship.

But just like a lone sheriff, love is no match for a whole gang of bad guys who come into town looking for a fight. Their evil and destructive intentions would be too much for one man to handle. The sheriff would be wise to hightail it out of town unless he is willing to go down in a blaze of gunfire. Likewise, love alone has little chance against today's automatic weapons that discharge distrust, disloyalty, and disrespect in a hail of relationship gunfire. Love will eventually have to seek refuge from any barrage of criticism, narcissism, or pessimism. The only way love will prevail is if we give it the relationship backup it needs. Be determined to give your love a fighting chance by giving your relationship "town" some solid citizens and weapons to work with.

Chapter Five

What is a Brilliant Marriage?

I think where people often get it wrong with marriage is in their expectations. People often talk about the "perfect couple" or how two people are just perfect for each other. We do this to a fault. We use terms like "match made in heaven" or "soul mates" to describe what we think is a standard. In the Christian world, we talk of how God brought us together and how it was "ordained" or meant to be. I believe this ideology sets up people for disappointment and disillusionment when marriages fail. So let me tell you what a brilliant marriage is not:

A brilliant marriage is NOT:
- A perfect marriage.
- A flawless marriage.
- A brilliant wedding day.
- A brilliant social media photoshoot.
- A brilliantly gifted couple.
- A marriage void of mistakes.
- A marriage without pain or disappointment.

A brilliant diamond reflects the maximum amount of light possible. That's just what diamonds do! Some diamonds reflect more light than others based on their characteristics. However, in every case, the light sources are critical because (get ready...) **no diamond possesses its own light**! It is essentially a reflector. You cannot see a diamond, no matter how perfectly cut, large, or clean, in the dark! A diamond's brilliance is based solely on its capacity to reflect light from an outside source. So, even if the diamond has flaws, some color, or is not cut perfectly, it can still possess a level of brilliance based on the light that is available for it to reflect. In the same way, a brilliant marriage should reflect the maximum amount of God's light it can on those around it. No person and no marriage possess their own light; it all comes from God. The problem we experience in marriage is thinking that either person is the source of light. This leads to unfair comparisons and criticism. But even if there are limiting characteristics in your individual life and marriage, you can and should reflect light. How much you reflect is up to you. Yes, you and your partner have a part to play in how brilliantly you shine for all the world to see.

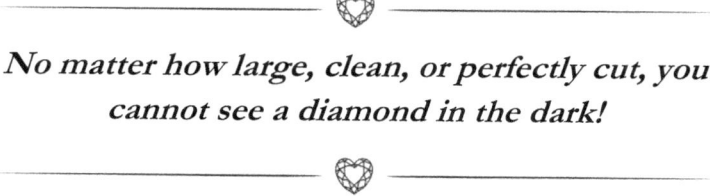

No matter how large, clean, or perfectly cut, you cannot see a diamond in the dark!

So, let's change the paradigm. Let's shift our focus from perfect couples, soul mates, and matches made in heaven as the standard for success. Those titles are often given in the early stages of a relationship when everything is going well. If that were the only criteria for success, nearly everyone would live happily ever after. I believe too much emphasis on being the "perfect match" can lead to a false sense of security. It may undermine the need to continue to make the relational investments needed in different seasons of marriage. You and your partner will evolve. Your needs will evolve. Your marriage will evolve. Your physical needs will evolve. The way you express love will evolve. I believe we should focus on how God ordained marriage to reflect his relationship with the church during every phase of marriage. The marriage relationship (not the wedding event) is supposed to be one of the ways God puts His grace, favor, and love on bold display.

If God had a social media account, he would post photos of married couples so they could be seen by the world at large, reflecting His glory. Though the light of love He shines on the marriage is perfect, the couple is not always reflecting that love completely. Sometimes, it is obscured by attitude, anger, and arrogance. At other times, it can be covered by pride, pain, and petty behavior. But despite our relationship foibles, flaws, and failures, He chooses to post less than picture-perfect marriages on Heaven's social media page in hopes that the light that is reflected is seen by others! He doesn't only post the perfect photos. He doesn't delete images from his heavenly timeline just because they don't bring him honor and glory. He is ever hopeful that even through rough times, his light will shine through the marriage relationship in a way that is brilliant!

The Four C's of a Brilliant Marriage

So, if there are four C's that give a diamond brilliance and lasting value, what characteristics, if any, will do the same for a marriage?

I am so glad you asked!

As a reminder, the 4Cs of a diamond are carat, color, clarity, and cut. When each element is top-notch, you will get a brilliant gemstone. It should be noted that the absence of all four characteristics does not prevent the diamond from being a diamond. It will always be a diamond. Its substance doesn't change, but its brilliance may vary. It will always have value, even if it does not have the highest value in everyone's eyes. This is because one of its greatest and most enduring characteristics is hardness, which serves it well in both industrial and laboratory settings. But most people want and value a diamond for the "bling," the visual appeal, and the brilliance. In the same way, a marriage without the following four C's does not cease to be a marriage or a functional, meaningful marriage relationship. However, it may lack the brilliance and value that appeal to or benefit others. Our goal in this book is brilliance! My observations over the years have led me to identify the four C's for a brilliant marriage as follows:

- **Covenant**
- **Communication**
- **Core Values**
- **Counsel**

You may disagree with my four C's, and that is totally fine. I would be more than happy to debate and discuss it some other time. But since you are reading my book now, my objective in the following discussion is to show you just how critical these attributes are in a marriage that is both radiant and resilient.

Chapter Six

Covenant

A covenant is defined as an agreement, usually formal, between two or more people to do or not do something specified. One of the places we see the prominence of a covenant is in the Bible, and more specifically, in the Old Testament. The word for covenant is "***Beriyth***" and refers to "*divine ordinance with signs and pledges.*" In my mind, a covenant is to marriage what a carat is to a diamond. It's the weight and substance of a marriage. In modern Western marriage, a man and woman are united through signs and pledges (exchange of rings and public vows), which gives the union "weight" and, therefore, worth or value. Apart from the biblical application, we recognize that any agreement between persons that is not verbalized, documented, validated, certified, notarized, or signed has no legal weight or value. A marriage covenant, in God's eyes, is the basis and foundation of marriage value.

Contemporary opponents of traditional marriage have often used the phrase, "It's just a piece of paper," when referring to the value of a marriage license or certificate. While it is true that a marriage license does not guarantee love, commitment, or marital success, it does document the agreement or commitment to the state. It's a form of natural and social accountability.

Interestingly, many of the same opponents are quick to establish legally binding prenuptial agreements on a "piece of paper" to protect their assets and hold their partners accountable for certain actions if the relationship breaks down! The problem is not what's on the paper; it's what's in the heart. Though a covenant on the surface looks much like a contractual agreement, the intent of a covenant is to establish and express a heartfelt commitment. A contract says, "I will commit to doing my part if you commit to doing your part." When one party doesn't fulfill their commitment, the contractual agreement is in jeopardy of being voided. Breach of contract and unfulfilled obligations can happen in business for a variety of reasons. The same is true of marriage partnerships. When people approach marriage like a contractual agreement, there will be several opportunities for obligations to go unfulfilled. Why? Because people mess up. People are fallible. People make mistakes, and sometimes they overpromise and underdeliver. As a result, there will always be opportunities for people to back out of the agreement because one party didn't do their part or do it in a satisfactory way.

If both parties have a covenant mindset, then they are committed to doing their part. Period. That is a foundation for success because their willingness to fulfill their responsibility does not depend on the other person.

A contract mindset says, "If you don't do your part, I don't have to do my part" in the relationship.

Covenant, on the other hand, says, "I am committed to doing my part even if you don't do your part."

God is the perfect example of the ultimate covenant keeper: He remains faithful to demonstrate His love and commitment to mankind regardless of what man does. This is the attitude and approach that men (and women) need to take in marriage based on the passage in Ephesians 5:33 (NIV), which states: *"However, each one of you also must love his wife as he loves himself, and the wife must respect her husband."*

Are You Covenant Ready?

I strongly encourage those who are considering marriage to closely examine the traditional marriage vows in advance and determine if they are up to making such a commitment. I have been to wedding ceremonies where couples purposely avoided declaring the potentially negative aspects of life in their marriage vows. They framed their vows to only make a declaration of good things and prosperous times in their future. Instead of saying, "for better or for worse," they would say, "for better or for better," and totally avoid mentioning sickness or poverty. Listen, I get that nobody looks forward to those things in life or in marriage. Nobody plans to be sick or poor. However, that is not reality. Life happens to all of us in a variety of ways. Sometimes, life comes at you faster and harder than you are prepared for. But how would you feel if the person who claimed they loved you "to the moon and back" made a vow that had an entire checklist of things they would never do? Can you hear them saying, *"I promise to have and to hold, EXCEPT for the times you have unexplained panic attacks, are unemployed for more than six months, suffer severe postpartum depression, go through a mid-life crisis, or generally can't seem to get it together?"* Nobody needs to get married if they are planning on loving only when the conditions are near-perfect in the marriage.

A covenant mindset is not just committed when circumstances are under control. They remain committed when circumstances are beyond their control. It is in times of conflict, crisis, and challenge that the power of the covenant is revealed. People often use the term "ride or die" and the phrase "until the wheels fall off" to describe enduring relational commitment. Though not perfect, these phrases attempt to capture the idea that nothing outside of us will separate us. Circumstances or external hardships will not break us up.

I believe that traditional wedding vows are designed to address the extremes that life will bring, the good and the bad, the highs and the lows. So, I want to encourage you to review the traditional wedding vows and ask yourself if you are covenant-ready for a future marriage. Also, if you are already married, you may not have gone into the relationship with a "covenant" mindset. It's never too late to change your frame of mind as it relates to the covenant.

The Wedding Vows

I _____, take you _____ to be my wife/husband, to have and to hold, from this day forward; for better, for worse; for richer, for poorer, in sickness and in health; to love and cherish until we are separated by death, or the Lord's soon return. As God is my witness, I give you my promise.

***

We are typically fine with the "having and holding" part. It's an amazing feeling to be wanted and valued by someone you love. We now have someone to be with on cold nights and lonely weekends. We have someone to be sexually intimate with. We have someone to cuddle and snuggle with. We have someone to accompany us to social events. That someone can also enhance our identity. We are clearly worth something to somebody because we were chosen by somebody to be married! It feels great to have somebody and to belong to somebody! So far, marriage is great!

When we think about the extreme positives of marriage, we are all in. Love, health, happiness, wealth, peace of mind, and prosperity are what we look forward to in marriage. We expect things to get better and be better together. The sky is the limit! We never expect to do worse. But when we consider the extremely negative possibilities of marriage, we might be inclined to step back a bit. We may be tempted to seek clarity on all this talk about for better, for worse, for richer, for poorer, or in sickness and health. We might be inclined to ask about what is meant by "in sickness and in health." Like, how sick are we talking? Are we talking about everyday flu symptoms, the black plague, or leprosy? Exactly how poor is poor? Are we talking about "third world" poor, soup line poor, or living check-to-check poor? The beauty of marriage vows is that they attempt to address the wide range of circumstances that people might experience as they live life together. The turbulent conditions of change that may blow in during the marriage will shake a mere contractual agreement. The legal term for outside forces beyond our control is "force majeure" – a French term that literally means "greater force." It is related to the concept of an act of God, an event for which no party can be held accountable, such as a hurricane or a tornado. In this case, all bets are off, and parties can go their separate ways without liability or consequence. Covenant commitment and love, however, are different. They endure and persevere through "forces beyond our control" until death do us part.

But What If?

Invariably, people will ask such hypothetical questions as, "What if?" or "What about this situation?" when the idea of covenant is discussed. They will say that there are exceptions to every rule and note that they have a friend who went through this or that situation. I can't possibly address every circumstance or scenario in this book. I won't even try. However, my point on covenant is the attitude of heart and mindset that both parties must embrace as they enter into a marriage relationship. This is not puppy love, boyfriend/girlfriend, speed dating, swipe left or swipe right, or dating relationship reality TV stuff. This is for grownups who are committed to the idea of a marriage that will last. This requires a measure of personal resolve. As noted, most people plan for the "best-case" scenario: endless sexual intimacy, solid financial standing, upward mobility, secure jobs, travel, and a spouse who totally understands and puts up with our "minor" or even major flaws. We never plan to develop bitterness, addictions, or bad attitudes. We don't anticipate losing jobs, losing hope, losing our tempers, or losing interest in our partner. We (hopefully) don't plan on falling in love with another person or having an affair with a co-worker. We don't plan for a spouse to develop a long-term illness. More importantly, we don't plan on seeing our partner ever change for the worse, develop bad habits, or have physical or emotional issues. We truly look forward to "happily ever after" without a plan for making mid-course corrections along the way. This is not to imply that engaged couples should plan for disaster, dysfunction, or drama. It simply gives credence to the truth that marriage should not be entered into lightly or unadvisedly.

Many couples find themselves both married and manipulated or wed while wounded. This is not God's intention for the marriage covenant.

To underscore the significance of a covenant mindset in the face of unexpected or unplanned circumstances, let me introduce you to Shannon and Shirley Austin. Together, they run a company called Marriage Inc. (www.marriageinc.us), where they provide coaching, a Masterclass, and other services for married couples. I have never met them, but I recently saw them on a podcast discussing some of their challenges in their 20+ years of marriage. During that time, both had been involved in extramarital affairs and had unhealthy relationship habits. However, the affairs were only the tip of the iceberg. Their website bio highlights even more challenges:

We have experienced the gamut of emotions, from the highest highs to the lowest lows. Our marriage has survived infidelities, hopelessness, financial deficits, near-death health scares, loneliness, constant arguing, years of being disconnected, and a near homicide/suicide. We lived in a negative and unhealthy cycle that we just couldn't seem to break.

Their experiences were not limited to external forces seeking to destroy their union but also to the internal forces they could not seem to overcome. A lot of couples can maintain the "two against the world" mentality when there is a visible, common external threat. But what if the threat to the marriage is INSIDE the marriage relationship? What if a partner's trauma, pain, fear, or dysfunction rears its ugly head during the marriage?

Ladies, what if you discover that the "strong, silent type" of guy you married is not just silent but completely incapable of constructively expressing his emotions or feelings? What if he only knows how to express his feelings through pouting, withdrawal, anger, rage, or destructive behaviors? What if the unpredictability of his expression keeps you walking on eggshells as you wait for the next violent eruption? What if you eventually become the target of that eruption? It's a huge problem when you feel physically and emotionally unsafe in your own marriage.

Fellas, what if the "trophy wife" you married and are proud to show off to your buddies is ONLY good for the show? What if the sharp tongue that made her seem clever and witty when you were dating has now become the razor blade that lacerates your manhood? What if you find that her penchant for "keeping it real" is really her thinly veiled excuse to administer small doses of verbal abuse that infect your decision-making ability with doubt and uncertainty? What if your efforts to display emotional vulnerability have been weaponized against you? What if instead of hurling words, she begins to hurl objects at you (yes, men get physically abused, too!) or threatens bodily harm? Just like with the ladies, it's a huge problem when you feel physically and emotionally unsafe in your own marriage.

There's no question that these types of internal marriage dynamics lead to separation and divorce among believers and non-believers alike. From a biblical standpoint, we know that God hates divorce (Malachi 2:16) and cites limited circumstances in which divorce is deemed acceptable (Matthew 19:8). This book is not advising you men to get divorced because your wife burned your breakfast. It is not telling you, ladies, to get divorced because he snores at night and makes you lose sleep. Her inability to lose the baby weight and his growing waistline are not reasons to get a divorce.

Unfortunately, there are marriages where one partner is resistant to change. They may not be open to working on themselves or the marriage relationship. They may be making life a living hell for their partner in a variety of ways. There is zero value in staying in a verbally, emotionally, physically, or sexually abusive marriage partnership just so you can say you stayed married. It's not a testimony to "stay married" while you are sporting a black eye, broken heart, and wounded soul.

Ladies, wearing a ring on your finger with his fingerprints around your neck is not a good look. Men, being esteemed by coworkers while being emasculated by a wife, is an unbearable conflict of the soul. Betrothed while being beaten, engaged while being eviscerated, married while being manipulated, and wed but wounded are not God's ideas for the marriage covenant. God does not get any glory when you stay married to a person who is draining you of the very life He died to give you.

What people so often describe as "irreconcilable differences" is often one or both individuals being unwilling to change for the sake of the relationship's success. So often, individuals would rather be right than be reconciled. Shannon and Shirley Austin have demonstrated that their willingness to be reconciled has led them to make the necessary changes to honor their marriage covenant. This has paid huge dividends both for them and for others. The numerous couples they have helped is the evidence of their resilience and radiance. Yes, in my opinion, their marriage is brilliant. They have shown that covenant is not about blind allegiance. It is about purpose. It is about intentional commitment with a divine result in mind. Notice that God had a purpose for everyone He established a covenant relationship with within the Bible. Even though the individuals may have gone through some challenging times, God's purposeful intention remained clear.

Chapter Seven

Communication

Communication is the lifeblood of any relationship. Without communication, there is no relationship. I know this firsthand because, as a sixth grader at 52nd Street Elementary School in Los Angeles, I finally got the nerve up to ask a girl to be my girlfriend. I only ventured to ask her AFTER several of my classmates told me that she liked me. I thought she was absolutely one of the prettiest and smartest girls in the sixth grade, and I was way out of my league. I asked anyway, and to my utter amazement, she said yes. So began our brief romance, which lasted only two days. That's right, two whole days. The reason it lasted only two days was because I popped the question during the last week of the school semester before summer vacation. During those two days, we would see each other in certain classes or between passing periods. We would smile and wave to each other from a distance on the playground.

However, I never talked to her on the phone after school; we never did homework together or even had lunch together. I can't recall if we had a real conversation. Then, over the summer, I never called her, never visited her house, or met anywhere to hang out. That's because I never thought to ask her for her phone number or her address. I literally had no idea how to be an elementary school boyfriend. Nobody told me what to do next after clearing the hurdle of asking her to be my girlfriend. Don't judge me; I was a naive and nerdy sixth grader.

Clearly, I was ready for the "idea" of a relationship (though largely driven by pre-pubescent peer pressure), but not an actual relationship. So, when one of my friends asked me over the summer if we were still boyfriend and girlfriend, I had to honestly tell him that I didn't know. She had not contacted me, and I had not contacted her. I didn't know if she still wanted to be friends or if she hated my guts. Unfortunately, after the sixth grade, we went to different middle schools for the seventh grade. So effectively, the last time I saw her was the last day of the 6th grade. I never saw her again. Did I ask her to be my girlfriend? Yes, I did. Did she agree to have me as her boyfriend? Yes, she did. But did we ever really have a relationship? I think it's safe to say that we didn't. It was all because we had little to no communication.

A dictionary definition of communication is *"imparting or interchange of thoughts, opinions, or information by speech, writing, or signs."* In various New Testament Bible passages, the word for communication comes from the Greek word "koinonia," which means *"fellowship, association, community, communion, joint participation, or (social) intercourse."* The root word *"koinos"* carries the idea of *"having in common, partnership, or fellowship."* Though the dictionary and Bible definitions sound somewhat different, the objective is an exchange for the purpose of sharing and partnership. So, when communication breaks down, understandably, sharing and partnership breaks down. Companionship, camaraderie, and communion breaks down. Information exchange breaks down, and the lives that were once united by thoughts, ideas, dreams, goals, and common interests are largely reduced to two individual lives once again. Once the two are separated, the dynamic power that could be available to them through their joint participation in a marriage partnership becomes effectively nonexistent.

The topic of communication is an extremely broad one, the complexity of which cannot be overstated. Even though our communication (exchange of information) is tremendously enhanced through technology, our communication (fellowship, community, and joint participation) is at an all-time low. In other words, as a society, we are talking and imparting information but not really communicating. Bringing people from different backgrounds, family structures, personal experiences, and world views together is no small task, whether it's for a school project or a corporate business exercise. When you add things like gender, age, and cultural differences, the complexity of communication increases dramatically, all this before discussing the challenges of communicating in a marriage partnership!

The beauty of a school or corporate project is that it usually has a clearly defined objective and a finite timeframe for completion. For example, building a solar-powered vehicle for an engineering design competition is a short-term project with a clear end date. Compiling data from various departments for the annual financial report is a clearly defined project with a clear end date. Marriage is different. Most married individuals don't have any idea of a defined objective aside from living together, having sex, raising kids, and retiring later in life. The end date of "till death do us part" can create problems for relationships because it's difficult to see that far ahead. By contrast, the school or business deliverable only requires you to play a specific role for a limited period of time. Often, there is less emotional attachment to the other people involved and once the project is over, you can move on to something else. You can go to another school or change jobs if you want to! Not so with marriage (refer to our discussion about covenant relationships). Marriage requires communication across every season and spectrum of life, especially in situations where the objective is not so clearly defined and the end date is seldom in view. These are just some of the reasons why communication in a marriage can be challenging.

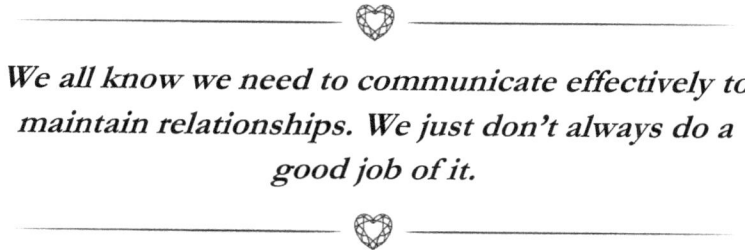

We all know we need to communicate effectively to maintain relationships. We just don't always do a good job of it.

We know that communication is a critical aspect of any marriage relationship, but we often underestimate our own inability to communicate effectively. As a man, I have become all too aware of my inadequacies in this vital area. It is generally understood that women communicate differently than men. Neither way of communicating is inherently good or bad. Just different. This is why a group of women can get together and be totally engaged in discussions about shopping, fashion, and hairstyles, while a man in that space might be inclined to check out. Alternatively, a group of men can talk about sports, guns, cars, and the like, and women would be inclined to leave them behind to go shopping! Certainly, the subject matter discussed makes a difference. However, another issue is HOW they talk and communicate in these spaces.

The seminal work by John Gray titled *Men Are from Mars, Women Are from Venus* focuses on the primary psychological differences between the two sexes. The bestselling book asserts that each sex can be understood in part by the distinct ways they communicate. Aside from the commonly held premise that men tend to be logical and women tend to be emotional, Gray makes several other key observations about the differences between male and female communication styles.

Some key differences to be aware of include, but are not limited to:

- Men tend to listen to a woman to "fix" a problem, while women want men to just listen to them. Period. What she wants is empathy, while he thinks she wants solutions.
- Women tend to want to "improve" the home, the man, or the way he does things. While he simply wants her acceptance, she thinks she is being nurturing. He can view her "home improvement" efforts as her being controlling.

Without digging up every possible difference, it is easy to see how miscommunication takes place in marriage simply based on gender alone. It might be a small miracle that it doesn't happen more! But aside from male and female differences, you may have observed several other ways harmful or negative communication can create problems in a marriage. These communications (or lack thereof) create more conflict than connections. They sap the marriage of unity, energy, and harmony.

Here is the shortlist I came up with:

Say What?

Sometimes, we say things to our spouses that we would never, in a million years, say to a co-worker or a person on the street. It's most often the case that familiarity breeds contempt. Maybe we take them for granted. Maybe it's that there is a greater consequence with a co-worker or a stranger. A co-worker might report our offensive words to the human resources department. A stranger might punch us in the mouth. But somehow, we expect our spouse to allow us to talk to them in a way that ranges from disrespectful to verbally abusive without consequence.

When you dim the brilliance of your partner, you effectively dim the brilliance of your marriage.

The fact is, we often treat our loved ones worse than coworkers, neighbors, or complete strangers. I have heard men talk to their wives as if they had a tail. I have heard wives literally talk to their husbands like they were children. Neither is acceptable. One of the easiest ways to dim the brilliance of your marriage partner is with words that degrade, demoralize, and demean.

Say Something!

Ladies, while you were dating, you found you were insanely attracted to the strong, silent type. The mystery and intrigue: the quiet brooding over issues captivated you. Now that you are married, the mystery has morphed into frustration and the intrigue into exasperation. When you ask him what he is thinking, you get nothing, and it's driving you insane. His unwillingness or inability to express his thoughts or feelings has left you feeling left out. You feel like an outsider in your own marriage.

The silent treatment is a form of psychological abuse used by both men and women to control the victim's behaviors.

Historically, we have heard that the strong, silent type was synonymous with a man under control. A man of few words has more impact when he does speak. But not this man. He has been taught by society that keeping his emotions under lock and key is a protective measure against those who would want to hurt him. He may be doing it as a response to childhood trauma or simply because the men in his life did the same. Either way, it's not healthy for your marriage, and it's not healthy for him. It is hard to express brilliance when a man finds it hard to express himself.

Say Something (Part 2)

Have you ever gotten "the silent treatment" from your partner? We all have times when we are offended or hurt and just can't bring ourselves to have a constructive conversation at the moment. It's okay to need some time to get yourself together emotionally and figure out how best to express yourself. However, purposely deciding to punish a partner by withholding words is a manipulation tactic. Withholding your words is effectively withholding yourself. When it is done for days or weeks at a time, it can be extremely confusing or painful and can make a person feel unseen, unloved, and unimportant. Using "the silent treatment" doesn't solve or resolve issues. It leaves the issues hanging in the balance until the victim bends to the will of the perpetrator.

The victim is often driven to capitulate to the will of the abuser to break the silence, restore communication, and feel "seen" or loved again. This only serves to further empower the abuser. It sends the signal that their tactics are an effective tool to get their way. Since people tend to do what works for them, they will use it again and as often as needed.

You Don't Say?

Some forms of communication are conveyed by the things you don't say. And trust me, people hear what you do say as well as what you DON'T say all the time! At least, that's what I have heard some wives say about their husbands. Some wives have expressed frustration over the idea that their husbands rarely or never give them compliments. This could range from being complimented for being a good wife, mother, cook, or lover. Often, the lack of affirmation for her beauty or physical appearance informs her that she is lacking in that area. This lack is only amplified if the husband is quick to compliment other women or, God forbid, those on TV and social media about their looks! In many cases, this is not intentional on the part of the man. It may be that he never considered how impactful his words were on her. Conversely, he may not have considered how impactful the unspoken words were either.

A man once confessed in a men's group that he would never think of publicly criticizing or talking negatively about his wife. At the same time, he realized that he seldom, if ever, praised or complimented her. It hit him like a ton of bricks that what he was NOT saying to her contributed to her lack of confidence in certain areas. If you were to ask him how he felt about his wife, he would have told you that she was great, fantastic, amazing, beautiful, bright, and more. The problem is that the way he feels about her is never communicated to her. He likely assumes that she knows how he feels. This is much like the old-school husband who was asked by his wife if he loved her. His terse response was, "Of course I love you. I married you, didn't I?" Just to be clear (for the guys who may have missed it), saying you love your wife on your wedding day is wonderful. However, she needs to know it and hear it from you throughout your marriage journey together. I don't expect men to go around doting on their wives every moment of the day, but I do expect that when given the chance, they will affirm her value both to others and to herself. It will go a long way toward creating an atmosphere where she can shine!

There are tons of books that address every aspect of communication, so I won't attempt to cover every situation that I can think of that can diminish marriage brilliance. But I am sure you can visualize how things like body language, tone of voice, volume, profanity, repetition, name-calling, a lack of eye contact, and physical distance impact communication in a negative way. We didn't even address how being argumentative, combative, indifferent, aloof, evasive, secretive, timid, apprehensive, badgering, condescending, accusatory, or self-righteous can influence and poison our communication. There are literally hundreds of ways to communicate, and as a result, relational connections can go totally wrong.

So, what should be communicated in a marriage? The Bible gives some guidance on what NOT to communicate in **Ephesians 4:29 (NIV)** as follows:

> *"Do not let any unwholesome talk come out of your mouths, but only what is helpful for building others up according to their needs, that it may benefit those who listen."*

So, if we simply focus on the opposite of what the Scripture says, we will use wholesome words that are helpful for building others up. We would speak about things that contribute to the life and vitality of the marriage relationship. This does not mean that you always have a happy-go-lucky attitude and an inspirational quote ready for your partner every day. It does mean that you might make more of an effort to focus on the positive rather than the negative, share more good news than bad, and speak of future possibilities more than problems of the past or present. With some effort (and maybe some practice!), we can change our communication habits. The work may manifest in overcoming the tendency to see the world through a lens of fear, failure, and fault-finding. Resist the urge to operate with a fixed and inflexible mindset. This new communication effort should hit three targets.

Communicate to yourself

Start by speaking life to yourself as a daily declaration or prayer. Communicate what you want to become or aspire to. What do you want to discover?

Communicate with your marriage
Continue by speaking about your relationship. Describe what you want it to become or look like, consistent with God's will, as a regular affirmation or prayer.

Communicate with your spouse
Let the language you use on yourself in your private time begin to flow into your daily conversations. Challenge yourself to communicate ideas and aspirations and see how they become part of the fabric of your relationship.

Chapter Eight

Core Values

In the world of physical fitness, the development of "core strength" is critical to proper body function. Your core stabilizes your body and facilitates balance, stability, and movement in any direction. Weak core muscles can lead to fatigue and make you susceptible to injuries. Core weakness also places additional demands on other muscles, which can lead to poor posture and back pain. In a similar way, "core values" tend to anchor and stabilize a person's motives, decisions, and choices. They keep you from making decisions that lead you to waste valuable time or cause personal injury. They keep you grounded and centered. And even when you are not actively thinking about or expressing them, your core values show up everywhere you go. Think of your core values as your "North Star" that keeps your life on a certain course. We most often become aware of them when we are faced with a critical decision or a crisis. They show up when we ask ourselves what really matters most in life. Our core values also tend to move us toward our purpose. Core values may include showing love for children, helping others, being organized, being financially sound, building a strong family legacy, exploring new places, having quality alone time, or having a love for physical activity. Core values are what you would express with or without a crowd.

In the context of marriage, people often talk about being compatible with one another. I believe the idea of compatibility goes beyond liking the same kind of music or art. I believe it is based on shared core values. I want to spend more time exploring core values, but first, I need to make what may seem like a sacrilegious statement to some: *"Shared values may be a better indicator of marriage resilience than shared faith."* There, I said it!

Let me explain. I believe that Christians mistakenly think that just because they share the same faith in the same God, it will lead to an enduring marriage. As a believer, I know that faith is important. In fact, it is critical. I know that 2 Corinthians 6:14 says,

> **"Do not be unequally yoked together with unbelievers..."**

And all of that! So, I do believe that as two believers connect in a relationship, a shared faith should be a foundational consideration.

Shared values may be a better indicator of marriage resilience than shared faith.

Have you considered that the expression or action of that faith can be very different from person to person? It can be expressed differently from one denomination to another. A person steeped in Church of God in Christ (COGIC) practices is going to be at odds with a person raised in a Lutheran or Presbyterian setting. There are as many permutations of faith as there are denominational differences. And with recent election drama from 2016 to 2020, we saw well-meaning Christian people on both sides of the aisle (liberal and conservative) go to war over issues and their candidates of choice. Their conservative or liberal values shaped how they expressed their faith when their faith should have shaped their values.

Another reason for differences occurs when the two people are at different places in their spiritual development. If a new believer is paired with a more seasoned believer, their faith expression, habits, and maturity will likely vary. Finally, some believers profess their faith "in name only" and wear the title Christian as an affiliation to a group or culture. But identifying as a Christian and conducting yourself like a Christian are two very different things. You can easily claim Christian beliefs but be lacking in Christian action! So, when crises or hardships come, the beliefs you claim to possess will be tested. What will rise to the surface in the crucible of adversity are not your theoretical beliefs but, rather, your deeply entrenched values.

Your values are more than clever sayings or quotes that show up on your social media timeline. They are embroidered into the fabric of who you are at the core of your being, hence the term "core values." But as we noted earlier, "Christian" relationships break up in similar numbers as non-Christian relationships. Have you ever considered why that is? I suspect that in a great number of cases, one or both individuals failed to live out Christian values to the degree necessary to sustain the relationship. From a theological standpoint, it's the difference between orthodoxy (beliefs) and orthopraxy (practices). This is why I place core values as part of the 4 Cs and not Christianity. Your core values will drive your actions more than your ascribed mental beliefs will. If we are honest (get ready for another sacrilegious statement), there are non-Christian couples who thrive more in their relationship because of the honest expression of their shared core values than believers who profess to share faith.

I became aware of the difference between "shared faith" and "shared values" as a college student. As a Christian, I was always told to find a Christian roommate. Why? Because Christian roommates supposedly share the same values. A non-Christian would likely not value your faith and would conduct themselves in a way that creates problems for you. Images of a roommate smoking, drinking, cursing, and having wild parties in our apartment came to mind. I could see them having girls over and generally tempting me to join in their fun while I prayed for strength to resist temptation on a daily basis. That was the vision I had in my head. My reality was different, however.

In my freshman year, I had two roommates. The good news is that we were all engineering students. The bad news was that one was a backslidden Christian who went to a club on many weekends. The other was a devout Jehovah's Witness who went to the Kingdom Hall every weekend. Did we have different values? Certainly. Did we periodically have robust debates over the Bible? Definitely! But what we did not have was blatant disrespect for one another. We paid our bills on time, communicated our plans, shared cooking duties, and generally kept the apartment clean. We even collaborated on homework assignments when possible. Christian people would ask me if I was going to finally get a Christian roommate the following year. I considered it for a while, thinking my life would magically become better with Christian roommates. That is until I visited some other Christians that I knew. They were also engineering students, and we even attended some of the same classes and the same Bible study. Their apartment, however, was something to behold. It was an absolute disaster. There were books and papers everywhere, dirty dishes, and half-eaten food in unexpected places. They were haphazard when it came to paying their bills on time. If "shared faith" was supposed to be an incentive to live with these guys, I was not seeing it at all. From all appearances, faith was off the table, as was the food! It was then that I realized the power of shared values to create a better environment for practical everyday cooperation over and against shared faith.

As I descend from my proverbial soapbox on this issue, I think this is one of the biggest oversights made by people who say they are in love with one another. Whether they are people of faith or not, they tend to maximize the importance of their feelings, emotions, and connections (which are not bad things) but minimize their deeply held values or belief systems. If you are only interested in a six-month fling, your core values may be easily obscured by the emotional excitement of a new relationship. However, your core values influence how you operate over the long haul. They not only influence how you operate in your 20's but will follow you into your 30's, 40's, 50's, and 60's. Aside from some life-defining events, they will likely stay consistent over time. If you love education and learning as a 20-year-old, you will value that as a 50-year-old. If you value social interaction as a 30-year-old, you will value it as a 60-year-old. If you value peace and solitude as a 40-year-old, it is likely that you valued it as a teenager, too.

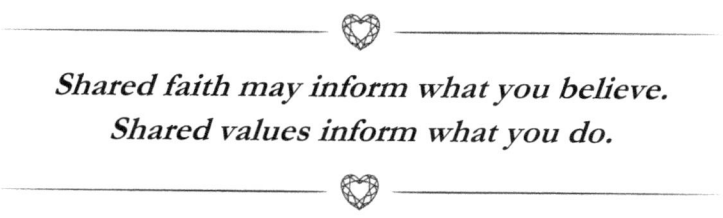

*Shared faith may inform what you believe.
Shared values inform what you do.*

In marriage and over the course of time, your core values will have more influence over the quality of your relationship in one way or another. If those core values are shared, they can lay the foundation for internal success and external influence. However, when individual core values are not shared, aligned, respected, or even acknowledged in a relationship, the result can be contention, bitterness, resentment, and insecurity. Expecting or pressuring a marriage partner to change their core values is a sure way to arrive at "irreconcilable differences" in marriage.

Corporate America Gets It. Why Don't We?

Corporations across the nation and around the world have come to understand the importance of articulating and modeling core values for their employees. Workplace engagement, harmony, and satisfaction can be directly linked to clearly defined core values. One of the benefits is that a person who does not share those values will either decide not to accept a position with the company or, after a short period of time, determine that they don't fit in with the company. I found the following paragraphs on Indeed.com as they relate to core values in the corporate space.

Core Values in the Workplace: 84 Powerful Examples | Indeed.com[2]

Core values are a set of fundamental beliefs, ideals, or practices that inform how you conduct your life, both personally and professionally. Businesses can also have and maintain core values. These can help an organization determine how to allocate resources, make important decisions, and grow.

People and companies typically select a set of ten or fewer core values to focus the ways they hire and maintain staff, approach daily business practices, and conduct communications. These values can inform how people interact (humility, respect, honesty), the focus of a person's or business' work (ingenuity, creativity, data-driven), or the individual responsibilities one will hold (consistency, quality, and reliability).

Identifying core values for yourself or within a company can provide structure and guidance, especially when dealing with a challenging decision or dispute. If one of your core values is honesty, for example, you would refer to it when deciding whether a certain piece of information should be kept secret.

---

[2] https://www.indeed.com/career-advice/career-development/core-values.

Companies recognize the power of operating with shared core values to maintain a positive work environment. So why don't we focus on shared core values in the closest relationship you will ever have in life? Don't get me wrong. I am in no way reducing a marriage relationship to a relationship between an employee and a company. However, beyond the romance, sex, intimacy, and excitement of loving someone and being loved in return, there is this thing called business. The volume of functional or business activities in a relationship that requires collaboration and decision-making far outweighs the romantic aspect – especially if you have kids!

All the business issues you had before marriage don't magically go away. They multiply! Everything from completing a degree program, working a 9-5 job, starting a business, changing jobs or careers, planning a family, choosing a church, selecting doctors and dentists, finding childcare, renting an apartment, purchasing a home, making renovations, paying income taxes, deciding on public or private schools, getting kids into extra-curricular activities and actually taking them to and from those activities (all day long!), PTA meetings, parent-teacher conferences, and helping with homework… can be exhausting! With all this day-to-day business, who in the world has time for romance? This is assuming you avoid mental and physical health breakdowns and don't have to take on the burden of managing other family members' issues! I didn't even get to the part where you must manage issues related to aging parents. We will save that discussion for another book.

My point is that a marriage will experience both the magical and the mundane, the momentous and the monotonous. Sharing core values will provide stability in terms of how these things are managed in a way that avoids conflict. For example, my wife is a giver. Generosity is a prominent core value for her. I always joke that she is so generous that she is willing to give people the shirt off my back! We were both raised to give and tithe regularly in our different church upbringings. So, there is absolute alignment in this area. This is not an area where a fight will break out in our household because of fundamental differences. I will admit that I am not as creative or "adventurous" around giving as she is, but I have no problem with giving if we have it and are not putting ourselves in financial jeopardy. In fact, I view her value of giving as an extension of our being able to bless others in spaces that I may not have been able to reach alone.

If I was a tightwad or didn't believe in biblical giving (some men forbid their wives to give to their own church), we would have conflict on a regular basis. As a result of my resistance to giving, she might be inclined to operate in secrecy or deception. My opposition to her giving might lead me to try to control the money or resources more. Neither of us would be happy nor free in that arrangement.

I could cover an entire list of areas where we are in alignment, even though one party may express their core values in a more prominent way. Even during our college years and long before pastoring a church became a reality, many of our shared core values were on display. Some that readily come to mind are:

- **Relational** – We have both always valued relationships with people over programs or prominence. Coupled with our generosity, it explains why so many people have lived in our respective homes with us over the years without paying any rent!

- **Teamwork** – We value being team players in marriage and in ministry. I don't need the spotlight and prefer collaboration wherever possible. I enjoyed being part of worship teams that collaboratively ministered to bring the presence of God into a space. Even though she is often asked to take on a leadership role or be a keynote speaker, she values working collaboratively to attain a stated objective. This is something she experienced while working on projects with Walt Disney Imagineering (WDI) for over 17 years.

- **Loyalty** – We are not quick to leave people, even when they act irresponsibly or otherwise (fill in the blank); we were in a previous ministry for seventeen years out of loyalty to God and to the people we were serving on the college campus. And the conditions there were far from optimal. In fact, they were often burdensome and oppressive. But we were committed to serving faithfully. So, being flaky in relationships is not in our DNA. However, when it was clear it was time to leave that ministry and the people we served, it wasn't out of a lack of loyalty to those people. It was loyalty to the call of God to start a new work.

- **Service** – We have a servant mindset. Regardless of the position or title we may hold in any space, we are not above serving to meet the need. We have both served in street ministry, juvenile halls, shelters, convalescent homes, and more. Service for us could range from being on stage to being behind the scenes. My wife has been on record saying that kids are not her ministry strength. Though she has spoken to dignitaries in different countries, I recall that during a ministry visit to an orphanage, she spent considerable time just holding a baby girl. We seek to serve to meet the needs of others.

- **Simplicity** – Neither of us is flashy nor extravagant. We prefer things to be simple. That doesn't mean we like things to be without quality or visible value. However, neither of us is drawn to or driven by what is outwardly gaudy or the mere look of extravagance.

The above is a short list of core values that have served us well both in marriage and ministry. There are others we may individually exhibit that are not shared to the same degree, but they are respected and valued by others.

God's Core Values

I would encourage any new or older couples to explore and discuss individual core values to discover and maximize places of alignment. It may be that you have similar values but different approaches. The conflict you are experiencing may just reflect different methods, not different intentions. Do your best not to get hung up on the method, but find ways to focus on the common objective.

Regardless of the core values you discover, I think it's important to know that God has the ultimate set of core values we should all agree on. What are they? I'm so glad you asked! Lest we forget, the Bible is largely a book about what God values. His values are conveniently summed up in the following passage in **Matthew 22:34-40**,

> *"[34] But when the Pharisees heard that He had silenced the Sadducees, they gathered together. [35] Then one of them, a lawyer, asked Him a question, testing Him, and saying, [36] "Teacher, which is the great commandment in the law?" [37] Jesus said to him, "'You shall love the Lord your God with all your heart, with all your soul, and with all your mind.' [38] This is the first and great commandment. [39] And the second is like it: 'You shall love your neighbor as yourself.' [40] On these two commandments hang all the Law and the Prophets."*

Jesus magnificently and succinctly sums it up for us as follows:

- Core Value #1   –   Love God with all your heart, soul, and mind.
- Core Value #2   –   Love your neighbor as yourself.

Sounds simple, right? Well, on paper, it is. Our unwillingness to internalize these values is where the problem often lies. I am confident that if we unpacked God's core values and investigated what it looks like to walk them out (orthopraxy) rather than just ascribe to them (orthodoxy), we would all be well on our way to a much more radiant and resilient marriage.

God's Core Values for Marriage:
Love God with all your heart.
Love your neighbor as yourself.

In conclusion, many individuals have a "list" of attributes they want their potential marriage partner to possess. The list for both men and women typically focuses on superficial attributes they find to be attractive. Again, there's nothing wrong with a list, but our short-sightedness and selfishness often render our list incomplete. In addition, if our list is framed by a response to trauma, loss, pain, and disappointment, we will most certainly value the wrong things. Unfortunately, if we don't discover our partner's core values during the dating or engagement phases, we will certainly discover them during marriage! In that arena, it's difficult to negotiate what values will dominate the marriage.

It is not the lack of core values that dims the brilliance of a marriage. We all have them. Instead, it is the vast differences in core values that lead people to file for divorce, citing "irreconcilable" differences. When people are not able to navigate those differences in a healthy way, it can lead to conflict. However, when core values are shared, aligned, or appreciated, they create a foundation of internal resilience and external brilliance!

Chapter Nine

Counsel

Counsel is the fourth C that I firmly believe is necessary for marriage brilliance.

I am a huge fan of couples getting some form of counseling before they get married. That's because many couples assume that their love for each other and excitement over their relationship will get them through any challenges. In some cases, one or both individuals don't want anyone in their personal business or telling them what to do. In the case of some older couples, they may feel that they have enough life experience to not require any counseling. They sometimes fail to understand that the accumulation of life experiences is precisely why they need counseling. The need for counseling applies to young people who will be experiencing married life for the first time. It also applies to couples who may be getting married later in life. It applies to individuals or couples who are remarrying after a death or divorce. Yup, in my humble opinion, it pretty much applies to everybody.

One reason I am so adamant is that I believe we all need a "second set of eyes" working for us. In my mind, the goal of counseling is not to run people's lives or control their relationships. It is to make them aware of personal and relationship blind spots. It also makes them aware of common marriage challenges. Finally, it is to make them aware of some "best practices" that they may choose to employ in their marriage. Though experience is a good teacher, oftentimes, it's less painful to let other people's experience be the teacher!

__Sound counsel can act as a "second set of eyes" to observe the blind spots in a relationship.__

Unfortunately, some couples see counseling as intrusive. I have heard people say that they are "grown-ups" and don't need someone telling them how to live their lives. Others don't want people judging their relationship or imposing random guidelines on their marriage. One online article on "Good Therapy - Find the Right Therapist"[3] observes that some couples dread counseling for fear of what might be revealed. Ironically, the

---

[3] https://www.goodtherapy.org/

problem areas they don't want to face before marriage will likely be amplified during the marriage.

Other couples don't give themselves enough time to get an appropriate amount of counseling. One meeting with a mentor, therapist, or pastor a few weeks before the wedding day may have limited impact and can be easily obscured by the frenetic and sometimes overwhelming wedding preparation process.

Taking Out the Garbage!

One of the benefits of counsel, especially before marriage, is that it cuts through all the garbage that has been fed to you over the years. You have been fed garbage about what marriage is and is not. If you are a man, you have been fed garbage about women. If you are a woman, you have been fed garbage about men. You have been fed garbage about yourself. You have been fed garbage about your family of origin. You have been fed garbage about your role in your marriage. You have been fed garbage about you, your partner, and your marriage by your environment, mainstream media, social media, your family, your friends, and yourself!

Now, don't get me wrong; you may be totally looking forward to a great marriage with a great partner, and that's a great thing! But you need to be aware of how random and unsolicited information may have influenced your outlook and perspective. For example, my wife and I had a great friendship before marriage, and despite my early mistakes, that friendship remained pretty much intact. We were both glad to be married to our best friend. However, we had been serving in a particularly tight-knit church for about six years prior to getting married. We also served in that same church for several years after getting married. Unfortunately, that church had some unhealthy perspectives on relationships and marriage. Even though we did not personally ascribe to their values, it placed us in an environment that would present challenges. So, during my engagement period, some of the guys (I won't call them men) in leadership would advise me on how to "check" my wife to get her to comply with my wishes. This "garbage" advice from unmarried guys was based on how they dealt with girls that they didn't even have a commitment to. When we got married, my wife would express her happiness with our marriage. Many of the women would counsel her to "just wait and see" until things changed. The clear implication was that she couldn't possibly be that happy in her marriage because they were not happy in theirs. It would just be a matter of time before "he" would change for the worse, and marriage would become drudgery. People who were married also uniformly said that the first year would be the roughest. Having heard that commentary a lot, I found myself mentally bracing for things to be especially "rough" in our first year of marriage.

I briefly imagined a turbulent environment, complete with temper tantrums and turf wars. It never materialized. It was not how we operated as people or related to one another. It was somebody else's garbage counsel based on their garbage experience. Don't get me wrong; we have had some passionate discussions, disagreements, and differences of opinion over the years. Still, it was nothing close to the marriage adjustment hell our "counselors" predicted for our first year or years of marriage. Take the garbage out.

Who's in Your Ear?

As I noted above, somebody is telling you something about you and your marriage at any given time. Back in our day (the 1980s), we didn't have 24-hour news outlets, millions of websites, numerous social media and streaming platforms, or hundreds of self-proclaimed relationship gurus giving unsolicited counsel all the time. So, you can avoid going to a reputable counselor all you like, but you are not going to avoid having someone in your ear ready to give you counsel. Everyday. All day long. Moreover, the problem is only amplified because every one of these "counselors" is working hard to get your attention. They have employed highly skilled professionals in many cases to find ways to get your attention. They are committed to having you listen to their message, and one of the ways they grab your attention is through shock and awe. They purposely craft a message or headline designed to pique your curiosity: Tell me more! Or to elicit a fight or flight response in you. Above all, if they "made you look," they have been successful. Now that they have your attention, they can tell you how all men are dogs and all women are gold-diggers and reinforce that message over and over. You may not believe the message totally, but now you can't unsee it. Subsequently, when you see it in real life and with your partner, it only confirms what your counselor has told you.

Baggage From Self-Counseling?

As pervasive and annoying as these counselors can be, they are not your greatest enemy. The greatest "enemy" counselor would be you! Yes, you are the one who is in your ear the most with your perpetual narrative about your life, your past, your failures, your mistakes, your insecurities, your pain, and your trauma. Because you believe in yourself so much, you will challenge others who believe differently about you, good or bad. If you are convinced that you are a complete loser, when others try to encourage you otherwise, you will fight them to affirm "your truth" about yourself. Besides, you must be right because you have amassed years of data to prove them wrong. Now, consider that your marriage partner has their own life narrative that includes their past, their failures, their mistakes, their insecurities, and their trauma. What you both have been telling yourselves (good and bad) will show up in your relationship.

I want you to get this picture.

Imagine you and your beloved on your wedding day. You are standing in front of an adoring crowd of friends and family as they lovingly smile and exchange chatter with one another about you and your partner. The wedding processional was spectacular, as the mothers were radiant and floated down the aisle to their seats of honor. The flower girl gracefully dispensed petals along the length of the runner as planned. The toddler ringbearer successfully negotiated his way down the aisle without distraction and safely arrived in the arms of the best man. Dad walked the bride-to-be down the aisle with a modicum of emotion and with a steady gait.

You and your partner stand at the altar before the minister. He has made his opening statements and prayed an eloquent prayer to set a tone of both solemnity and celebration. As you stand under a beautifully crafted arc of colorful flowers, it is time for you to exchange vows. You both do so with a touch of emotion as you consider the gravity of the moment. You then exchange rings designed to symbolize the precious and unending love that will be shared between the two of you for a lifetime. Just as the beautiful and awe-inspiring ceremony is set to conclude, you both make one more exchange. Behind you both is an oversized, old, tattered, and worn piece of luggage that is bursting at the seams. You both grab the handle of your respective bulky baggage, awkwardly drag it from behind you, and then set it before the other person.

This unexpected exchange represents all the things that you have accumulated, collected, and gathered for years in advance of this sacred day. All the expectations, fears, lies, beliefs, hopes, dreams, deficits, insecurities, trauma, damage, distrust, distress, and dysfunction you have lugged around are finally being presented to the person you believe can help you shoulder the load. But there is one problem. You are unloading your luggage on them, only to have them unload their luggage on you! Your burden will not be suddenly and magically lifted. You will not be instantly relieved. Wouldn't it be great to have known about this baggage exchange before the wedding day? Wouldn't it have been useful to be able to open the baggage in advance to examine what was inside and decide whether it was of any value to your future life and marriage? Even if some unpleasant items needed to be kept, it would be beneficial to have some strategy for dealing with them.

In addition, the size or weight of the luggage that you decide to share will not blindside your partner. They would be able to prepare for the road ahead. Or, in another scenario, they may decide before getting married that they are not up to the task. This might be a reason to decide that marriage is not the best move for now or ever.

As much as this last alternative may sound like an unpleasant or painful rejection, it may spare two individuals from having a more painful marriage experience. It may also spare them from having to divorce when much more is at stake. Sound counsel from seasoned marriage mentors, a therapist, a counselor, or a minister is an indispensable tool to help you prepare for a journey called marriage. Can it identify and solve every possible problem in advance of a wedding? No. However, it can inform both parties about the potential problems, pitfalls, and potholes ahead, so you have a greater opportunity for success.

Chapter Ten

Dirty Diamonds and Blurred Brilliance

Having identified the various facets that make a brilliant marriage, we must also pay attention to some of the things that compromise potential brilliance. Diamonds and people tend to get "dirty" with exposure to the elements. Our environment can impact our ability to shine despite our good plans or intentions. The only way to keep a diamond from getting dirty is to keep it locked away in a jewelry box. The only way to keep marriage partners from getting dirty, scarred, or wounded by the world we live in is to bubble wrap, ziplock, or seal us to prevent any human contact. We can always choose complete isolation, but that's not how we are designed by God to operate. We don't have much control over the environments that we find ourselves in, whether it's the workplace, family, or community. However, we do have a say in how we adjust to, manage, or respond to those environments.

Blurred Brilliance!

A new pair of white Air Jordan sneakers in the shoe store are immaculate. New cars that have advanced technology to go along with that "new car smell" are something that everyone loves. As consumers, we are enamored with new things! However, over time, novelty and new car smells wear off. Shoes wear out and go out of style. Cool new gadgets soon become outdated or obsolete.

Diamonds are different. In fact, the slogan "diamonds are forever" has a lot of truth to it. Their natural hardness ensures that they don't tend to show signs of wear and tear. The simplicity of their beauty ensures that they won't easily go out of style. Aside from a catastrophic event, the carat, color, clarity, and cut won't change. Diamonds tend to maintain their value over time.

However, their brilliance can be blurred or diminished. Their brilliance can be compromised because of external factors such as the atmosphere they are exposed to. For diamonds that are worn as rings, they may be exposed to everything the hands are exposed to. That includes body oils, dust, dirt, grime, perspiration, lotions, makeup, or chemicals. The accumulation of any of these things on the gemstone or in the setting will diminish the amount of light that passes through it. And as we know, the less light that gets through, the less brilliance we will see. So, what are the things that can blur the brilliance of a marriage? Good question. Since the four characteristics that lead to brilliance begin with the letter C, so do many of the things that blur brilliance.

Dirty Diamonds and Blurred Brilliance | 115

1. Competition

One sure way to blur your marriage brilliance is to compete with your partner. I am not talking about the kind of competition that spurs growth and engagement. Playing competitive board games, working out together, and setting personal goals are great places for friendly competition and challenge. I am talking about your attempts to always outshine your partner by diminishing their brilliance. I am talking about competition that seeks to win at all costs, often at the other person's expense. One definition of "compete" is *to strive to outdo another for acknowledgment, a prize, supremacy, profit, etc.* This sounds a lot like the TV show *Survivor*, where the stated purpose is to "outwit, outplay, and outlast" the other contestants for a prize or 15 minutes of fame. If your marriage is a perpetual rerun of *Survivor*, it likely will <u>NOT</u> survive to see another season. It's only a matter of time before the "competition" becomes ugly and any marriage brilliance is lost forever.

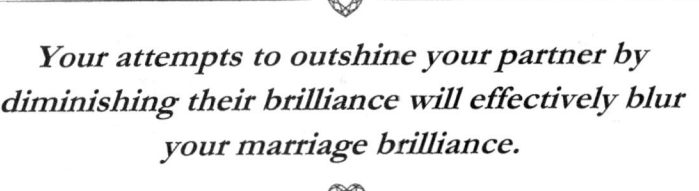

Your attempts to outshine your partner by diminishing their brilliance will effectively blur your marriage brilliance.

I believe both marriage partners are designed to be winners together and to shine together. For those who truly need to conquer something, they should look outside of the relationship.

There is a whole world out there with problems and issues that need your "conquering" energy. And if you and your partner can join forces in conquest over life issues and challenges, you will be on your way to marriage brilliance!

2. Comparison

There is a popular saying that goes, "Comparison is the thief of joy." Well, if marriage partners are constantly comparing themselves against one another, there probably isn't a lot of joy in the relationship. If competition identifies winners and losers, comparison identifies what is better or worse. One person may cook, clean, manage money, or organize better than the other. That's fine. That's normal. That should be expected. The identification of who has the best gifts, talents, and skills is not wrong. It can help determine how best to utilize or leverage your resources. However, using comparisons to measure a person's contribution (or lack thereof) to the relationship can become a source of conflict. It's a way to keep score. Further, comparison to determine a person's worth or value is a problem. This "value" is often articulated when a person identifies what they "bring to the table" in a relationship. Clearly, the **contribution** of each partner is critical to relationship success. Contribution can be a matter of expertise, education, or effort. But comparing to determine who is better or worse, worthy or unworthy, is a losing proposition. Let's focus on how we can both best contribute to our relationship going forward and restore our joy!

3. Complaining

To complain is to express dissatisfaction, resentment, or grief, to find fault. We will all have complaints about our partners from time to time. We will be dissatisfied, let down, or disappointed. We will find fault. That's human. But a complaining attitude is different. This attitude was evident with Moses and the children of Israel in the Bible (Exodus 16:7-9 NKJV). God could literally do the miraculous, and yet people still complained about what He did NOT do. For the complainer in a marriage, nothing is good enough.

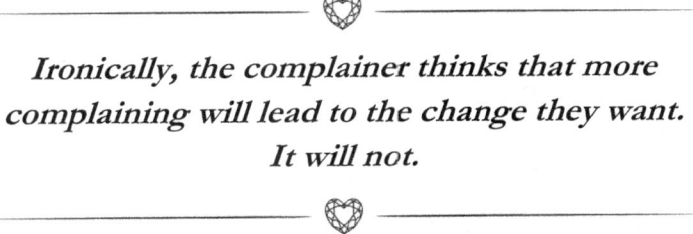

Ironically, the complainer thinks that more complaining will lead to the change they want. It will not.

Even if things do change, the habit of complaining remains. Complaining also has a profound effect on the one complaining. Some studies show that repeated complaining rewires your brain to make future complaining more likely.[4] Independent psychology researcher and author Steven Parton once penned an article titled "The Science of Happiness: Why complaining is

---

[4] The Science of Happiness: Why complaining is literally killing you. – Curious Apes

literally killing you." In the article, he notes that with every thought, "The brain is rewiring its own circuitry, physically changing itself, to make it easier and more likely that the proper synapses will share the chemical link and thus spark together—in essence, making it easier for the thought to trigger. This "rewiring" precisely is why complaining becomes a habit for some people. Over time, you find it's easier to be negative than positive, regardless of what's happening around you. Complaining becomes your default behavior, which changes how people (and your relationship partner) perceive you. If complaining is killing you, it is also having a similar effect on your partner.

4. Criticizing

Complaining and criticizing go hand in hand. They both work together to tear down and create a negative atmosphere in any relationship. To criticize is to find fault and judge unfavorably or harshly. As we noted earlier, every relationship has both facets and flaws, dimensions and imperfections. We all have ample opportunity to criticize our partners based on our respective differences or defects. My wife revealed to me on several occasions that my penchant for not locating the closest or "best" parking spot used to bother her. She was tempted to criticize. However, she ultimately realized that it was not worth it. Not finding the perfect parking spot in a mall does not need to be elevated to a relationship emergency. The energy (and potential arguments) over what parking spot is selected would almost never be productive. The most important thing is that we arrive at our destination and park safely. The same can be said for a variety of issues that we can easily criticize one another over. Take a moment to consider if the criticism is helpful to the relationship or just a gripe that you want to express. Of course, all criticism is not bad. Using criticism that is constructive, helpful, and leads to solutions is the ultimate objective. It should be grounded in love and based on truth if it is to be effective. This is what creates an environment where brilliance is possible.

5. Complacency

Another thing that blurs marriage brilliance is complacency. This can be defined as being pleased with oneself or one's merits, advantages, or situation, often without awareness of some potential danger or defect. This is a classic in many marriages. The level of effort people put forth to develop a healthy romantic relationship tends to wane over time. People sometimes take their partners for granted. Priorities get rearranged. Life happens, and often, people make subtle adjustments to accommodate dysfunction.

I have been guilty of marriage complacency – being pleased with my situation without awareness of potential relationship danger. I was unaware of her dissatisfaction or frustration. I was so complacent that I was defensive about my complacency! It doesn't mean that I did not love or appreciate my wife. I settled into the marriage "routine," and that was fine with me. On the other hand, my wife wanted adventure, new experiences, challenges, and fun. She wanted greatness. I wanted routine and safety.

One sign of complacency is when you realize that you are saying "no" to any new ideas or experiences far more often than you are saying "yes" to them. Complacency by one partner is one of the ways distance is created in marriage. When people say, "We just grew apart," it is often because one person moved while the other person stayed still. It's because one person was growing while the other remained stagnant! When one or both parties become complacent or stagnant, marriage brilliance is bound to become blurred.

Brilliance Blockers

I categorize things that blur marriage brilliance as those that dim or diminish the light that God wants to shine through a marriage relationship. They are often rooted in some level of selfishness, insecurity, or fear and may have a cumulative effect over time. Brilliance blockers, on the other hand, are things that can obscure or block out the light that should radiate through a marriage. These most often deal a severe or fatal blow to the marriage relationship and damage the people involved.

Cheating

It seems that nearly every TV show that has a relationship includes an element of cheating in it. Extramarital affairs, trysts, entanglements, and "situation-ships" have been normalized. Movies often use extramarital affairs as the pivotal or inciting incident in a story. Social media skits almost always use cheating as the primary source of relationship conflict or distrust. Hollywood often depicts cheating as an "affair," a "fling," a one-night stand, or the result of a moment of passion. They don't call it fornication, adultery, whoredom, unfaithfulness, or any of those serious-sounding Bible words. *Side note: my spellchecker said the word "whoredom" might be considered offensive to some readers. Point taken.* They focus on the intrigue, the secrecy, the stolen fruit, or forbidden pleasure. They paint the picture of a stable relationship as a boring or mundane prison that the cheater is desperate to escape from. Being stuck in a relationship with a predictable partner often justifies the cheater's actions. The element of cheating, however, in TV or movies is an effective tool to engage the audience emotionally. It creates tension and conveniently gives us someone to root for and someone to root against. We automatically get both victims and villains delivered to us for our viewing pleasure. In some cases, we are led to root for the cheater because their horrible, boring partner deserved to be cheated on. That's the Hollywood version of cheating. Its immense relational impact is conveniently wrapped up in a 30-minute sitcom or hour-long episode. Infidelity issues are magically resolved in a 120-minute movie. The cheater is glamorized, their impact is minimized, and the act is normalized. But that's far from real life.

The real-life version is not so simple. To take a cue from a Hollywood movie title, I would say *It's Complicated* at best. In real life, there is trauma on many levels. Infidelity can have lasting impacts on partners and children.

In the Hollywood version of cheating, the cheater is often glamorized, the impact is minimized, and the act is normalized. But that's far from real life.

Grief, physiological and emotional changes, awkward behaviors down the road, and mental health conditions such as anxiety, chronic stress, and depression can occur as a result of cheating. No movie can accurately capture the tears of regret shed over any period. No feature film can effectively address the painful life decisions that have to be made to reconstruct a fractured family. Discovering, investigating, or exposing a cheating individual is merely the tip of the emotional iceberg. The deception leads to an unending cycle of accusation, blame, questioning, doubt, and suspicion. Ultimately, every extramarital affair leads to three key results:

i. Casualties

A casualty is a person or thing that is injured, lost, or destroyed. Even though every affair has a "villain" and a "victim," both parties are casualties of an affair. Both parties lose something in different ways. Clearly, the victim will be directly hurt, wounded, or traumatized by the lies, secrecy, and betrayal of the person they loved. Their ability to love that person or another person in the future may be lost or destroyed. The villain (cheater), though responsible for the marriage rift, will experience guilt, shame, remorse, and the loss of love and trust. If they don't feel the sting of their actions, it is because they have become indifferent or calloused to the person they cheated on for any number of reasons. If they justify the cheating and lack remorse, their hardened attitude is yet another loss.

ii. Consequences

"Consequence" is something produced by a cause. It is a result or an outcome. If an Olympic athlete is caught cheating on the biggest stage in the world, the potential rewards, reputation, and relationship losses will be great. Those losses may be felt for years to come and even have a long-term impact on their quality of life. In the same way, the cheater in a relationship (villain) may suffer shame, embarrassment, and a loss of reputation. If kids are involved, they may be dragged through divorce court to deal with child custody issues that impact a salary. Most people would say all this is well deserved.

The "victim" will have a million questions, all while going through the grieving process repeatedly. Aside from the emotional roller coaster, there is the impact of financial and household instability and the prospect of fighting for ownership of joint possessions and accounts. None of the material or financial issues will be resolved without significant expense, thanks to the court system and legal profession. I could go on and on with specific outcomes from cheating, but I am confident you get the point. You probably have several examples you can cite from experience or memory. You may even be carrying the receipts for cheating in your back pocket. Even though there are exceptions, there is a lot of truth to the saying that cheaters never prosper.

iii. Collateral Damage

In war, the killing of civilians in a military attack is considered collateral damage. In an affair that leads to separation or divorce, the children are the ones most often damaged. They were neither the primary combatants nor the instigators of the conflict. They were simply innocent bystanders. Yet their young minds and hearts are often exposed to an onslaught of insults, disrespect, and volatile behavior between parties. Even though they may not be privy to court proceedings that impact their future, the collective vitriol between parties does not go unnoticed by children of any age.

    I have a friend who is an attorney. His practice involves representing marriage partners who are embroiled in the divorce process. He often shares how painful it is for him to watch couples who were once in love completely eviscerate one another over issues related to visitation, custody, money, material possessions, and children. As legal negotiations escalate, the simple objective of raising healthy children is obscured by efforts to paint the other party in the worst light possible. The husband quickly becomes labeled a deadbeat dad, and the wife is tagged as an unfit mother. This child's or children's relationship with either parent is permanently altered, as is their view of marriage. The damage children incur is often incalculable. To a lesser degree, friend groups, social groups, and family connections are damaged, altered, or dissolved in the process. In many cases, they may side with one party or the other based on their viewpoint, bias, or preferences. This is not what they signed up for when they were witnesses to the former couple's marriage vows.

Cheating (Part II)
Though people often justify these other forms of cheating as being harmless, they are not. They still violate the marriage vow and potentially block out the light designed to reflect through the marriage relationship.

i. Emotional Affairs
Emotional intimacy outside of marriage can do as much damage, if not more, to a relationship as a physical affair. This can occur between co-workers or the soccer mom and dad, where proximity, frequency, and shared interest are key factors. It can be marked by:

- Spending more time talking to or thinking about that person rather than your partner.
- Sharing personal feelings or information that you don't share with your partner.
- Knowing they're attracted to you or knowing you have "chemistry" together.
- Feeling less physically or emotionally attracted to your partner.

The impact of an emotional affair is particularly challenging, even if there is no sexual contact involved. That's because the painful consequences of a partner's emotional cheating – the sense of being deceived, betrayed, and lied to – are still present. Trust that has been violated in any way takes time to rebuild.

ii. Pornography

In the old days, you had to go to the corner liquor store to buy a Playboy magazine. Today, pornography is accessible not only on TV but to virtually anyone via computers, tablets, smartphones, and a variety of social media platforms. I have heard people justify the use of porn by saying that it doesn't hurt anybody. Nothing could be further from the truth. Unfortunately, I have first-hand experience (and receipts) from an online porn addiction that literally blocked my personal brilliance and that of my marriage. I cannot adequately describe the sense of betrayal and hurt that my wife felt over this issue that I brought into our relationship. The broken trust and broken promises she endured took their toll on her in ways I never imagined. What's worse is that initially, I justified it, minimized it, and accepted it as part of life that I did not believe I could overcome. The deception many believe is that they can stop at any time. The deception I believed was that my love for my wife would give me the power to stop. It did not. The truth is I didn't love or value myself enough to stop. Simultaneously, the weight of the guilt and shame I carried did a number on my confidence and my character. Brilliance blocked. The weight of holding a secret and the fear of being confronted or exposed impacted my thinking.

The underlying themes common to pornography, emotional affairs, chat rooms, phone sex, sexting, and any other digital or cyber-cheating are secrecy and self-deception. The secrecy and lack of disclosure create a fertile environment for distrust in the relationship. One of the direct results of distrust is relational distance. The offended party is pushed toward self-protection and self-preservation, which is counter to two becoming one or two being better than one. The offending party is pushed toward more secrecy, deception, or justification. The act of shining light on these dark areas, though extremely uncomfortable, begins to open the door to operating in your personal and relational brilliance. Failure to allow the light of truth to flood these areas effectively blocks the light that God designed both for you and your marriage to reflect.

Control

Control is defined as exercising restraint or direction over to dominate or command. Unfortunately, this takes place in some form or another in many marriages. When God created man, he gave him the capacity to dominate. Genesis 1:28 says:

> *"Then God blessed them, and God said to them, "Be fruitful and multiply; fill the earth and subdue it; have dominion over the fish of the sea, over the birds of the air, and over every living thing that moves on the earth."*

Though control of his environment is within God's design for mankind, the directive to "dominate" does not include other men or women. Let me say that in a different way for those in the back.

God never intended for men or women to dominate or control one another. Yes, history and various cultures have been built on patriarchal systems that view women as second-class citizens or even property. This has never been God's heart. When he created Eve from Adam's rib and called her a "suitable helper," it is commonly understood that she was not to be beneath him but beside him. She is to be beside him in principle, purpose, and practice; beside him in collaboration and conquest. Unfortunately, the ongoing "battle of the sexes" we see is a direct result of the fall. This competition or desire to rule is a byproduct of the sinful state of mankind in a fallen world. We see it played out in corporate culture, on TV, in movies, and on a variety of social media platforms.

God never intended for men to dominate, control, or enslave men or women. Similarly, in a marriage relationship, God never intended for the man to dominate or control his wife.

It is not uncommon in marriage to see people attempt to control a person through verbal, emotional, physical, and even sexual abuse. Other ways include withholding access to financial resources, monitoring daily activities, and preventing interaction with friends or family. My wife and I had some friends who were newly married in their early 20s. In some cases, the wedding dream quickly turned into a marriage nightmare. In one instance, a husband sought to instill fear in his wife by holding her over an apartment railing several floors off the ground. Another husband, to control his wife's activities, took her car keys to prevent her from leaving the house. To double down on his threat, he then proceeded to throw them as far as he could – several hundred feet away – into the shrubbery of a neighbor's backyard at night. This husband never considered the difficulty of her trying to recover the keys so she could go to work, the store, or take their kids to the hospital in an emergency. The other husband never considered his wife suffering a severe injury or death from such a fall. He never considered her children being raised without a mother. In his need to demonstrate supreme control, he never entertained the idea of going to jail for such an act of cruelty. Both men's only objective was to satisfy their momentary need for control through the use of dominance and fear.

Both women bore multiple children to their abusive husbands. This is one of the factors that the men leveraged to reinforce the wife's responsibility to marriage and family. Though both wives were subjected to continual micromanagement, unreasonable demands, and criticism, they were both academically and intellectually astute women. Despite their relationship challenges, both women managed to pursue advanced degrees and career advancement. They eventually left their spouses, not because they didn't believe in marriage or submission. They left because they believed that they deserved better treatment from men who called themselves Christians.

Many people have suffered untold abuse in controlling marriage environments. The effects of domestic abuse and violence are staggering today. Some of those effects include worsened psychological and physical health, decreased quality of life and productivity, and even mortality. According to the National Coalition Against Domestic Violence (NCADV.org), it is estimated that 1 in 3 women and 1 in 4 men have experienced some form of physical violence by an intimate partner. Moreover, 1 in 7 women and 1 in 25 men have been injured by an intimate partner.

There are numerous studies and resources that address relationship violence and abuse. I will not attempt to address them in this book. However, this is where I want to underscore the need for one of the Four C's – counsel – mentioned earlier.

Counsel

Individuals outside the relationship typically have a more objective view that is not clouded by emotional or sexual attachments. They can often pick up on controlling behaviors the couple cannot or is not willing to see. The saying that "love is blind" is not completely true. However, the emotion and excitement of a budding relationship can have blinding effects on a person's judgment. It can create blind spots or lead us to overlook a partner's insecurity or need to control a relationship. Efforts to manipulate, dominate, or control show up in a variety of ways, including but not limited to a combination of gaslighting, micromanagement, being overprotective, dictating your decisions, isolating you from friends or family, criticizing, and blaming. Seeing these elements early in a relationship should give a person a reason to either proceed with caution or "exit stage left" before committing to marriage!

Part III:
Fire

The "fire" in a diamond refers to the flashes of spectral color reflecting from a diamond's interior when it is moved while exposed to light. It is the dispersion of white light into rainbow colors because of refraction, the bending of light as it passes from one transparent material like water or glass to another. So, when a diamond has fire, you will get glimpses of a variety of colors, just like you see in a rainbow or a water spray from your garden hose. In the same way, every marriage can display a wide range of "colors" because of the way God's light shines through the couple. No couple is designed to be monochromatic or without color. When God's sovereign purpose is expressed through a couple, there will be glimpses of light that attract and even captivate onlookers. In the case of diamonds and marriages, "fire" is the result that we want.

Fire doesn't just happen. Every diamond that is formed in the earth under extreme heat and pressure does not automatically display fire. But every diamond mined from the earth has the potential to display fire. When the raw gemstone is subjected to the cutting process by a skilled jeweler, then its potential can be realized. As noted earlier, the process involves removing diamond material and reshaping the stone so it can capture and reflect the maximum amount of light.

In our personal lives and marriages, we all carry extra or unnecessary material. Often, we are emotionally attached to what we carry. We identify with our size, shape, and overall look. The cutting process represents change. It represents a loss. It is often uncomfortable. It may seem destructive. It will change your dimensions, shape, and size. Sometimes, it is due to an unwelcome outside source. Other times, it is the result of hardship or inconvenience. It can also be a direct result of being married to the person we fell in love with. Regardless of how it comes, we tend to whine about our discomfort and mourn our loss. But God knows that some parts of us need to be cut away so that the light can effectively pass through to create fire. His intention is to help us cut off those excesses. The ultimate outcome is a "fire" that is both visible and appealing.

Chapter Eleven

Private Brilliance

A Brilliant Marriage doesn't just happen. "It takes work." I find it encouraging that some already believe in putting in the work to get the desired result in any area of life. When it comes to developing a skill or a gift, we must put in the work. When it comes to building a business, we must put in the work. When it comes to raising productive children, we must put in the work. Likewise, when it has to do with having a brilliant marriage, we must put in the work.

It is disappointing that there are some who still think that their choice of a partner will automatically become a match made in heaven or that their marriage relationship will always be heavenly, without commitment to work. They often assume that just because they found their "soul mate," they will always "feel" that deep connection. But in reality, a soulmate can quickly feel like a cellmate without the proper amount of work. The problem is that we don't account for life's realities. We don't account for trauma, loss, or death. We don't account for misfortune, distress, or catastrophic events. We don't account for male or female hormonal changes. To be clear, the work is not because either person is bad. The work is because we are still growing, evolving, developing, maturing, and, yes, aging! Things can become familiar and routine. We can become jaded, cynical, and suspicious. We can become overwhelmed by life's challenges. We can be distracted by vain pursuits. Everyone reacts differently to stress or pain. It took me years to understand that, though I was often physically present, there were seasons and times when I was not emotionally or relationally present for my wife or kids. If my marriage lacked brilliance, I had to admit it was sometimes because of me. As the song says, "It's me, it's me, oh Lord, standing in need of prayer." In addition to "standing in the need of prayer," I could also stand to put in some work!

Putting in the work to enhance your brilliance can take place in several ways. Let's state the obvious. Any person created in the image of God can display brilliance. Believers in Christ have the capacity to reflect His presence in their lives. I make this distinction because a believer should be inclined to purposely yield to God's direction and guidance in life and allow Him to shine through them. So, I want to share three ways we can "bring brilliance" into a marriage without putting pressure on ourselves to do any superhuman feats.

Presence

Simply deciding to be present for your spouse often speaks volumes. Hopefully, the reason you are together is that you want to be *together*. The Bible states in Ecclesiastes 4:9 (NLT) that "two people are better off than one, for they can help each other succeed." Couples that end up living separate lives under the same roof are simply not maximizing their collective brilliance. For whatever reason, they have elected not to be present with and for one another. I mentioned earlier how, in a particular season, I found myself saying no to certain social events my wife wanted to attend more often than I said yes. By my own admission, I was a stick in the mud! In retrospect, making an effort to be present with her could have shown support in the same way we show support for our children who participate in sports or a dance recital. We don't do it only because they are superstars or play the leading role. We do it to affirm their value. Though your spouse is not a child wearing a baseball jersey or pink tight and a tutu, they are on your team. They are valuable, and as a result, what they do has value, even if it's not your thing. Make the most of every opportunity to be present and show the support they desire.

Preparation

So often, we prepare the most for the people we love the least. Preparation tends to communicate how much we care about or are invested in something. We apply it to proposals, projects, and presentations all the time. We want to put our best foot forward. But when it comes to our spouses, we often prepare "sloppy seconds" for them. Because of complacency or taking them for granted, we let our hair down (and I mean all the way down!) in their presence. Things you would never do on a first date, you now do with regularity. It could range from personal hygiene to physical appearance, wardrobe choices, cooking a meal, or failing to welcome them home from work with a smile and a hug. It could be neglecting to send a midday text message to prepare them for a night out after work without the kids. I totally understand that we can't be "on 10" every moment of the day. It's not realistic for most of us to look like a TV couple every day of the week. And if you have kids, sometimes the level of insanity is overwhelming. With kids, it's often more about perseverance than it is about preparation!

But how would it make your spouse feel if you prepared yourself for their arrival from a business trip or event? Instead of greeting her in that dingy t-shirt (and accompanying body odor) you just played basketball in, maybe cleaning yourself up and smelling good for her would be a welcome change. Conversely, instead of subjecting him to a vision of a hair bonnet and house coat, maybe give him a vision of the woman he would take on a date. As I am writing, I am reflecting on some of the times that a little bit of preparation could have made my wife feel more appreciated after a long business trip. Once, her response to my bland, distracted, and aloof reception of her after a lengthy trip to Africa was that she might as well turn around and stay away even longer. Ouch! I was so distracted by what I was doing that I did nothing to prepare for her return or to show I was excited to see her make it home safely. Lesson learned! It doesn't have to be a full-on ticker tape parade or a Broadway production every time your spouse comes through the door. In many cases, preparation is simply some amount of forethought or intentionality. It could be a card, a balloon, a banner, or flowers. It can be lighting their favorite scented candles or running some bath water. Simple and intentional acts can help a person feel important and thus bring brilliance to the relationship.

Participation

One of the most effective ways to cultivate connection is to participate in the thing or endeavor that your partner values. Where presence may simply require you to spectate, participation requires you to... well, participate! This is when you go beyond being with your partner when they do something and do the activity with your partner. So, they want to take up ballroom dancing to live out their *Dancing with the Stars* TV show fantasy? Why not participate in some classes with them? Do they want to learn axe-throwing? Why not participate with them? I can hear you now. It's not your thing, and it doesn't interest you. But if it's their thing and you are interested in them, what's the worst that could happen (assuming you don't have an encounter with an angry axe-thrower)? That's precisely what new couples do. One decides to share in the experience because they want to be with their partner. My wife once took up hiking some local trails to get exercise. She invited me to participate on several occasions. I politely declined several times, not realizing that her intent was to carve out a different type of "together" time. Go ahead and call me clueless because I only viewed it as something I did not want to do. I figured I could get exercise in different ways, even though I was not in the habit of exercising at that time. This was a missed opportunity to participate because, after a while, she stopped asking.

Other opportunities to participate may be in home improvement projects, making vacation plans, taking neighborhood walks (a family favorite of ours during the pandemic), reading books, or binge-watching TV shows. The thing I was most guilty of was NOT sharing in the activity because it wasn't "my thing" or because I had decided that my wife didn't need my help. In many cases, I took the stance that many men take during wedding planning. In most cases, a man is just not into all the details of selecting colors, napkin designs, and party favors. He may often feel his input will be trivialized or overlooked by the bride, wedding planner, and mother of the bride. So, it's easy to disengage and avoid participation. However, to some degree, his participation speaks of his investment and care. It speaks of his willingness to contribute, communicate, and provide constructive feedback. So, even if he wants periwinkle blue and they ultimately choose lilac, the very act of participating says, "I am present, engaged, and willing to roll my sleeves up and contribute."

A Precious Purchased Possession

During traditional marriage ceremonies, there is a time when the couple exchanges rings. Most men spend a considerable sum of money on an engagement ring and wedding ring set. It is not a small or insignificant purchase. Even on the wedding day, its care is entrusted to the best man for safekeeping. Upon the exchange of rings, the minister will often refer to the symbolism involved in the ritual. Much more than the exchange of jewelry, the rings connect the relational, emotional, and symbolic values of the marriage relationship. The ring is an unbroken circle and represents an unbroken circle of love–from God to man and from each marriage partner to the other. The ring is also typically made of precious metals such as silver, gold, or platinum. Just as mankind places great value on these precious metals and the rings exchanged, God places great value on individuals. They are exchanging hearts. They are exchanging their love and commitment. They are sharing the most valuable thing they possess themselves. Being made in the image of God, both parties are of equally great value in God's sight. Both are a unique and precious possession purchased by God.

When people exchange rings during a wedding ceremony, they are also exchanging the most valuable thing they possess – themselves.

Just as the rings should be treated with care, the people involved should also be treated with care. We would be horrified if the future bride casually spoke to her girlfriends about her ring as if it were cheap or worthless. We would be appalled if we heard the potential groom talking to the fellas about his ring as if it were a sign of bondage or a source of constant irritation. As hard as that is to imagine, it is not uncommon to hear some women belittle their husbands in the presence of their girlfriends. It is not uncommon to hear a man disparage his wife around his buddies. Worse yet, when tensions are high, they may even deride one another face-to-face without remorse. No marriage partner, created in God's image, should be treated with such disdain. I honestly don't think most couples start out with that level of disrespect in mind. But as time passes, words once laced with honor become words that hurt. If we have the presence of mind to regard the value of a diamond ring for a lifetime, why do we find it difficult to regard the value of the person we say God gave us for a lifetime? We take specific measures to show that a piece of jewelry is precious. Shouldn't we at least do the same for our marriage partners? Of course, we should! Is it always easy? Of course, it's not. That's why you are reading this book!

Treating your partner with great care and admiration is usually easy during the dating or honeymoon phase. Both parties still want to put their best foot forward and are thrilled that someone wants to be in a relationship with them. In these early seasons, it is usually easy to see the partner as a special gift. In addition to being in love with them, we may be blessed by the status, success, or security they add to our lives. We may find their simplicity or sincerity refreshing. However, over time, the "new car smell" of the relationship can wear off for various reasons! Sometimes, what was fresh and new becomes predictable, routine, or familiar.

At other times, the thing that was great when it was new eventually became a nuisance. What was once a privilege, over time, becomes a problem. The old saying, "Familiarity breeds contempt," is true in any relationship and especially true in marriage. The idea is that as time goes on, people have more time to learn things they dislike about their partners. Add to this the fact that our consumer-driven lives are wired to crave new things, and you have a recipe for dulled relationships. So, where a co-worker may think you are the best thing since sliced bread, the marriage partner may see you as a stale slice of bread far past its expiration date. They see your mishaps, mistakes, and messes. They see you more undressed, unrehearsed, and unprepared than your co-workers ever will. Things like showing up for important meetings and events, providing courteous and timely responses to requests, and following up on assignments are all great workplace practices. Surprisingly, sometimes these same qualities don't follow us home! Maintaining your brilliance largely involves simply taking care of the relationships you have by following the Golden Rule: *Do unto others as you would have them do unto you.* With that said, let's look at protecting and polishing our marriage's brilliance.

Protecting

When a man thinks of protecting his wife, the image of a knight in shining armor fending off evil adversaries comes to mind. One aspect of protecting requires the ability to confront outside physical threats. Picking up a baseball bat in the dark of night to investigate strange sounds requires a certain amount of courage. It's relatively easy to kill the spiders, flying insects, or (God forbid) the occasional rodents that may invade the home, giving her every reason to flee to the nearest 4-star hotel. However, it takes a different set of skills to protect and cover her emotionally. This may include times when we must protect her integrity, character, and reputation.

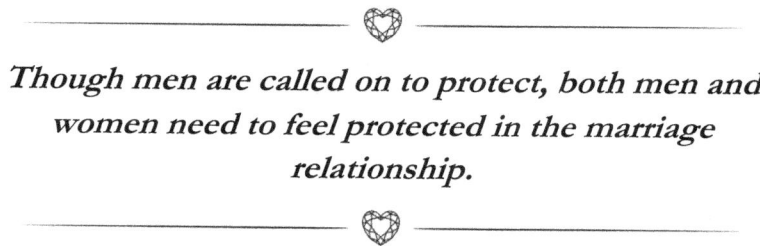

Though men are called on to protect, both men and women need to feel protected in the marriage relationship.

Recognizing when my wife was in emotional distress, in need of my support, or knowing what to do when she was overwhelmed required a different sensitivity. It also required me to move out of my insecurity or indifference. It required empathy–the ability to put myself in her shoes and advocate for her if necessary. Even though I loved my wife, it didn't guarantee that I saw things from her point of view or processed things the same way she did. I believe the key to a woman feeling protected starts with a man's proximity and presence. Being close and being available even if you don't have all the answers goes a long way to making her feel protected! When a woman feels unprotected, it opens the door to emotional distance, pain, distrust, and other factors that may place a wedge in the relationship. In summary, protecting is more nuanced than just whacking things with a hammer or emptying a can of bug spray on a creepy, crawly critter. It requires a different level of sensitivity and awareness of her challenges.

A man needs to feel protected in the relationship as well. Even though we don't envision our wives punching out the person who stole our tools or left a dent in our new car, we absolutely need our wives to protect us. Sometimes, we need protection from ourselves! The tendency to operate out of pride, ego, or insecurity can drive us to say and do some stupid stuff. Some very wise women have kept many men from making potentially life-altering mistakes. A wife's words or presence can give him a reason to avoid being overly aggressive or reckless. Though I wasn't reckless physically, I was pretty good at blurting out insensitive comments in public settings. I didn't do it to attack or embarrass anyone. Sometimes, I tried too hard to be clever or impressive. At other times, I was unable to "read the room" before making a statement. I recall times when my wife's gentle nudge under the dinner table prevented me from saying some things that I would later regret. Her soft squeeze on my arm let me know that I was about to tread on dangerous territory.

Aside from protecting me against social embarrassment, my wife has protected my feelings. There are times when, in her disappointment or anger towards me, she could have easily piled on accusations, observations, or revelations about my behavior that would have broken me down. Don't get it twisted fellas;

most women have the receipts for all your blunders and the verbal capacity to eviscerate you with great skill. If we are honest, we can look back on the many times that our wives have protected our name, reputation, and honor, both privately and publicly. That, my friend, is a gift from God!

Polishing

Polishing jewelry serves the purpose of cleaning to restore luster or brilliance. Routine polishing by the owner is necessary due to repeated exposure to corrosive salts, chemicals, and dirt that combine with oils on your skin to form a dulling residue. In this case, it is best to use a soft cloth that can remove the residue without scratching or marring the surface. In some cases, however, polishing requires the use of chemicals to restore brilliance. In the case of tarnished silver, the jewelry can appear to be dark gray, brown, or even black! My daughter once had a silver bracelet that turned dark brown because it was exposed to high sulfur content from the water in her apartment. To restore its luster, I had to expose it to other substances, such as salt and baking soda, to reverse the tarnishing process. The same is true in marriage. We need to first stop exposing our partners and relationships to the elements that rob them of their brilliance or luster. Those elements may include negativity, criticism, harsh words, and disrespect. More passive, yet just as dangerous, are things like indifference, nonchalance, disengagement, or being dismissive towards your partner.

Words of affirmation from our partner can often be the polish that helps us shine brighter!

To counteract the relational "chemical reactions," in most cases, doing the opposite is effective. Replace negativity with positivity, harsh words with kind words, etc. Introduce or re-introduce respect and praise where disrespect and criticism once took center stage. Though diamonds don't react the same way to the chemicals that tarnish metals, the principle still applies. Rather than using harsh chemicals or an abrasive cloth that will mar the surface, using a gentle cleaner and a soft cloth will usually bring back brilliance. Establishing positive elements that polish the relationship will effectively reverse the process that caused the dullness in the first place. The act of affirming your spouse, even for everyday things, sends the message that you indeed see and acknowledge their contribution. This can increase their personal sense of self-worth and even be a source of motivation. We do this with our kids most of the time, from encouraging them to take their first steps to praising them for their role as vibrant Christmas trees in the school's holiday play. Grown folks are no different.

Be the Jeweler in Your Marriage

The characteristic of a brilliant diamond that a jeweler truly has the most control over is the cut. One may argue that man can also determine the carat size or weight, but there are natural limitations to diamond size. Rough diamonds can come in unpredictable shapes and sizes, so the diamond cutter will create whichever shape maximizes carat weight and value. Though there are formulas that specify the number of facets that will provide maximum brilliance, the cut angles and depths can vary. In the same way that a jeweler should possess certain skills to cut a diamond, we need certain skills to influence the brilliance of our relationship. Now is a good time to see yourself as a master jeweler poised to bring brilliance to your marriage by developing or strengthening your skills.

Attention to Detail

Every jeweler worth his or her salt must pay attention to small details to create amazing items. In the same way, your capacity to create brilliance is increased when you pay attention to the details of your partner's life. Though this goes both ways, it is typically the man who is challenged in this area the most. You may have been the guy who never notices when your wife changes her hair color, nails, or dress. Those days need to end effectively today! One way to let her know that you notice the details of her life is to make an effort to notice the details of her life and say it out! Even if she doesn't always give you a gold medal for noticing things that concern her, in the back of her mind, she will appreciate being seen.

Since women tend to notice details more readily, it may not take as much effort for them to develop this good habit. Notice when he is stressed, emotionally fatigued, or distant. Notice how his mood changes and what things bring him peace. Notice him making an effort to do better, be better, and acknowledge it.

In both cases, noticing the good things needs to be acknowledged or verbalized so your partner can know that you notice! Also, in both cases, your "noticing" powers should be used for good and not evil. Do not, I repeat, DO NOT only notice so you can nag or nitpick! Catch them doing something good and let them know, rather than catching them doing something terrible and dwelling on it.

Steadiness

Every jeweler must have a steady hand to work with precision, often under a microscope. Without a steady hand and control, the proper cuts will not be made in a way that maximizes brilliance. In the same way, a marriage partner should exhibit a level of steadiness, composure, and control, even in challenging situations. These qualities give each partner greater confidence and security. There is nothing worse than having to work around the impulsive, haphazard, or capricious actions of a marriage partner at critical times. The goal is not to be predictable to the point of mind-numbing boredom but rather to provide your partner with a range of expected behaviors that elicit their confidence.

I recall a situation early in my marriage wherein my wife was extremely passionate or angry about a situation and proposed several dramatic actions she should take. For the record, she is not typically overly emotional or haphazard in her actions, so this was a rare occurrence built up by frustration over time. For the most part, she was just venting. Uncharacteristically, I chimed in with her and was willing to double down on her threats. I think I was trying to be emotionally engaged and supportive. She didn't see it that way. She promptly informed me that I was supposed to be the "steady" and rational one in the relationship. We couldn't BOTH afford to be "dramatic" on this occasion. In short, she felt comfortable expressing a wide range of emotions at that moment but fully expected me to provide the logical or emotional balance in our marriage. We later joked about how the results of us both being overly emotional or impulsive in our actions would likely land one of us in jail. In both our marriage and ministry, she has been the primary risk-taker, visionary, and "outside the box" thinker. I have no problem with that. She simply sees things I don't see. This gives me great joy to know that she can confidently trust that I will provide a stable and firm foundation for her. If you think about it, every rocket ship needs a firm launching pad before it takes off to explore outer space!

Visualization

A great jeweler needs to have a vision for the finished product before making a single cut. He must be able to see the result while looking at a stone that would not sell for much in a jewelry store. This ability does not come into play so that you can try to chisel your marriage partner into the shape or image you want them to have. This ability comes into play when you are called to pray for your marriage partner to become the person God calls them to be. You need a healthy, "God-centered" vision for your marriage and your marriage partner. It is utterly useless to try to make them what you want them to be because their primary purpose on earth is not to serve you. But to serve God.

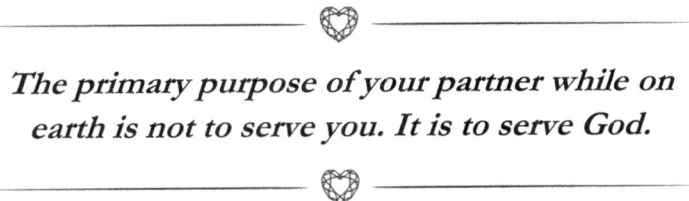

The primary purpose of your partner while on earth is not to serve you. It is to serve God.

So, your objective should be to help them develop into the brilliant person that God wants them to be. That will be the most glorious version of the person you married and the person that will enable you to collectively fulfill God's ultimate purpose in life! As you discover your partner's quirks, idiosyncrasies, passions, and gifts, you may find yourself uncomfortable at times. But oftentimes, you are seeing the seeds of the very thing for which God proposed them to do.

One of the situations where I learned to lean into who my wife was called to be was discovered while we were shopping for a car. I am a guy who doesn't like window shopping. If I don't have the money to purchase something, I may as well stay at home until I can. So, when we were interested in purchasing a new car, we went to a lot and casually looked at sticker prices. I knew we weren't going to buy anything that day, and she did, too. But as soon as the salesperson came over, she not only engaged him, but she also began to negotiate with him! We even sat down and began to fill out paperwork, and they checked our credit. As I watched this process unfold, I was momentarily terrified that my wife, knowing full well that we were not ready to purchase, would put us in a position to buy a car! Then, when the salesperson left to get the manager to "seal the deal," she said we should play the "good cop/bad cop" game. In this case, I would be the unimpressed, resistant husband, and she would be the "all too eager to purchase" wife. I had absolutely no problem playing my role and saying "no" to every offer or "best deal" the salesperson put on the table. Ultimately, we did not buy a car. But we did leave with the knowledge of how low the dealer would go to sell us the car.

My wife's penchant for negotiation and deal-making was on full display that day. That same ability has served us well as we moved into ministry and leased, renovated, and later purchased a three-million-dollar church building. If I had insisted that she fulfill my vision for her as a wife, she would never fulfill God's vision for her as a leader! I am really hoping the men who hear this *really* hear it. Some of the things about your partner you don't understand may very well be indicators of how God wants to use them for things outside of your marriage! Clearly, this goes for women as well when it comes to their husbands. My wife has always been quick to pay attention to my interests and support me accordingly. In a season before kids were a thing in our lives, I was part of a church worship team and led worship for our college Bible study. I decided to start learning to play the piano to expand my musical capabilities and for personal pleasure. Let me cut to the chase. I am not a great piano player to this day. I never developed the discipline or focus to become a great piano player. I mostly tinkered around with it for my own enjoyment. And once we had children, there was little time to use it as an outlet or get away from the challenges of life. Yes, I sometimes believed I could have become a great musician! For a while, however, the piano became my obsession, to the point that my wife called it "the other woman" in my life as I tried to plunk out different worship tunes. It turns out that I was playing on a cheap electronic keyboard, which was fine with me. Even I wouldn't have invested in something pricey, given my limited piano expertise.

So, rather than complain about my musical preoccupation, she got me a better and more expensive "other woman" for one of my birthdays. Even though the keyboard provided some level of competition in terms of how I used my time, she saw the value of my interest. Maybe she secretly hoped I would excel or simply wanted me to be happy with an enjoyable hobby. Either way, her vision for me led her to support me rather than oppose or try to change me. Luckily, my brief piano love affair did pay some dividends. I began to better understand some things about chord progressions and how songs were constructed. This served me well when leading worship at church or at men's conferences for many years after we had kids.

My point is that often we will oppose our partner's peculiar interests, passions, or curiosity when we don't understand. When it doesn't seem to fit our vision for how we want them to show up in our lives, we may see it as something we must try to change. However, if we were to get a glimpse of God's vision for their lives and how He wants to use that gift or peculiarity in our lives, we would be less inclined to pick a fight over it. A good jeweler has a vision for the unfinished gemstone that the consumer does not have. That's exactly what I believe God would have us be for our marriage partner – a jeweler with a vision from God regarding our marriage partner!

Chapter Twelve

Public Brilliance

The world needs your unique brand of brilliance. Even if you never walk the red carpet or stand on a stage before thousands of adoring fans, the world needs the unique brilliance that only your marriage can bring. I believe that you, as a couple, are designed to fill a void, answer a question, or meet some need in your world. It may be local or global. It may impact the community or influence the country. It may be for a season, a generation, or a lifetime. I mentioned earlier that one of the core values my wife and I shared was a heart for ministry. It didn't matter where we were on earth; we were going to serve in our local church in some capacity.

Prior to starting our church in September of 2003, we had previously served in our college campus Bible study at California State University Northridge. We quickly went from simply attending to serving and ministering. Her primary gift was preaching and teaching, while I felt called to lead worship. In addition to those functions, we did everything in between, including sharing our faith with students, inviting friends, leading prayer groups, setting up and serving food, giving students rides home, and more. During our 17+ years of being committed to the Bible study group, we transitioned from being students ourselves to being the double income, no kids (DINK) leaders, mentors, and de facto "parents" in that environment. Thankfully, we were privileged to be the only Bible study leaders who were married and owned a home then. So, our house became the place where students came to get fed, hang out, get mentored, or get some tutoring if we knew the subject.

One young lady frequently came over to escape her dorm roommate and have a quiet place to read and study. Her quiet presence became so normal to us that she blended into the household scenery. Rather than go home after her classes were over, she would come to the house and find a quiet spot on the couch or use one of our spare bedrooms to study in. She would leave late at night, only to return the following day. For her, our home was a refuge. Other students came and went over the course of time, and we gladly fulfilled their needs for food, conversation around God's Word, or resolving roommate and relationship conflicts. I recall that the foot traffic in the house left the carpets in continual need of cleaning. We also began to realize that our home was too small. Not because we had a growing nuclear family but because we had a growing number of students and their friends coming through on a regular basis. So, in 1998, we bought a larger house.

When we finally felt compelled to leave the church (which had become toxic) and the Bible study at the end of the fall 2000 semester, our decision was not announced beforehand. But for some strange reason, many of the 75+ students gave us cards or notes thanking us for essentially being their pastors while they were away at school. They saw something in us that we didn't see in ourselves. I think they saw brilliance. It was pretty unexpected and quite humbling.

The students saw something attractive in how we ministered to them as a married couple and made them feel like family. They saw brilliance!

By the spring of 2001, having left the previous church, we were passionately moved to start our own Bible study on the same campus. We called it **"HOPE Fellowship."** This was not to show the other church that we could do a better job or to compete with them. It was simply our heart's desire (and core value) to continue to minister to an entirely new set of students on campus. We still wanted to connect students to a version of Jesus and faith in God they may not have gotten from their moms' or grandma's traditional church experience. We wanted them to grab hold of their own faith for themselves! We wanted them to experience the HOPE, OPPORTUNITY, PURPOSE, and ENCOURAGEMENT that we knew could be found in Jesus Christ.

After starting with just a handful of students, by the spring of 2003, the group was again pushing towards one hundred people.

Unexpectedly, as summer drew near, many students who would be staying in Northridge over the summer began asking us to have a church service in our home. They mentioned that gas prices were too high or that they lacked transportation to get back to the Los Angeles area for the church. Though we thoroughly enjoyed ministering to college students, we had zero aspirations of starting a church or having church services in our home. We didn't see it at the time, but this new set of students saw brilliance in us, too. They saw something attractive, desirable, and eye-catching in how we ministered to them as a married couple and made them feel like family while they were away from their own home.

At their urging, we reluctantly (but prayerfully) decided to have one church service in our home. Just one! I opened with worship, and my wife preached the sermon. To cap off the Sunday experience, my wife also cooked a traditional soul food meal the night before that we served after church was over. So, the students were fed both God's Word and good soul food. Some even stayed and took a nap after eating. It felt like a great success, and I'm always grateful for that experience to this day!

In our naivete, we thought they would be happy with that one service. That was not the case. They wanted more because they saw a different level of brilliance in our marriage and ministry. I don't want to imply that we were the best church service in the world or on par with any established preachers or institutions. But for those students, and at that time, we met their needs in a tangible and unforgettable way. To them, it was brilliant because brilliance (like beauty) is in the eye of the beholder! So, after a week or two off, we had church services in our home again.

Over the summer of 2003, we eventually held services on a weekly basis. After much prayer, deliberation, and planning, we formally launched what is now known as H.O.P.E.'s House Christian Ministries (www.hopeshouse.com) in September 2003. And by the way, the young lady who regularly came over to escape her dorm roommate to read or study became one of our thirteen founding church members! She went on to graduate from CSUN with honors, teach special needs children, and eventually obtain a doctorate degree in her field of study. She is just one of the many "success stories" that have benefitted from our marriage and ministry. By no means do we take credit for her academic or professional success; she had her own drive and put in the work to make it happen. However, to be able to create an environment for students like her to thrive away from home was both an honor and a blessing. It is in being a blessing that we discovered our brilliance even more. You can, too!

I am confident that we have not set any records for the biggest, fastest-growing, or most impactful Bible study or church. Our intention was never to be the most impressive, politically influential, or culturally relevant church. I know that I am not the most innovative worship leader (I don't have formal musical training) and certainly not the best singer. My wife would quickly tell you that there are multitudes of more prolific preachers than she is. Still, I firmly believe that our brilliance as a married couple and in ministry is embedded in our authenticity. In September 2023 (as this book is being penned), the H.O.P.E.'s House church celebrated 20 years of ministry in our community. During the anniversary, hundreds returned to celebrate with us even though they had started new lives, careers, and families elsewhere. I believe this was because they discovered authentic community and developed lasting relationships. I believe they discovered and experienced brilliance.

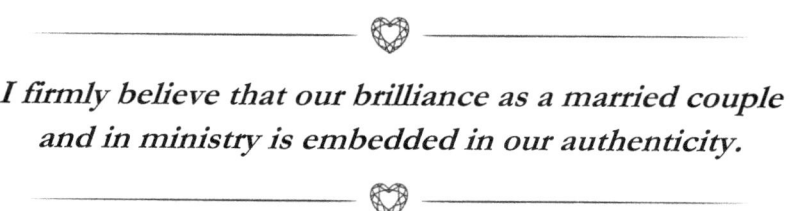

I firmly believe that our brilliance as a married couple and in ministry is embedded in our authenticity.

Our true value to others comes from just being who we are called to be, fully embodying our God-given identity and purpose. So, taking your brilliance to the world is not about setting records, achieving greatness in the eyes of the world, or being the "ultimate" at anything. Your personal brand of brilliance includes providing solutions to the problems God allows to arise in your marriage. It involves you adding value to the lives you encounter. It is about making yourself available to God so He can impact others through you. Your God-designed brilliance is unique to and for you and perfectly suited to meet the needs of others.

Your area of brilliance may not be ministry. However, you may have several areas where your brilliance is on display. It may be discovered while serving underprivileged youth or running a dance school. It may be working with seniors or teaching financial literacy. It could be in coaching or creating memorable music, art, or films. It may be keeping your community clean or helping people clean up their credit. There is no end to the number of ways your marriage can impact the world around you or the world at large when you allow God to shine His brilliance through you. This doesn't limit both individuals to doing the same thing all the time in the same space. However, you do need to be a supportive partner in the process and in every season. One or both of you may be in the spotlight at any given time. There will be times when both may not be in the spotlight at all. Each of you may be in different spotlights for a different purpose during different seasons of life. Just like there is no one way to describe the greatness of God, there is no one way to display your marriage's brilliance.

Historically, in many Christian circles, the image of the dutiful wife at home raising children while the man was out tackling the world to provide for the household was the norm. The woman was an extension of his good or bad reputation and name in the community. Her identity was tied much more closely to his success or failure, wealth, or poverty. As more women in the workplace have ascended to higher levels of influence in corporate America, sports, academia, and politics, they can more easily make their own mark apart from their husbands. In some cases, the woman may have a wider influence or public appeal. In a brilliant marriage, this should not foster competition but rather collaboration. When one rises higher, both rise higher. The Bible puts it this way in **Ecclesiastes 4:9-12,**

"Two are better than one, because they have a good reward for their labor. For if

they fall, one will lift up his companion. But woe to him who is alone when he falls, For he has no one to help him up. Again, if two lie down together, they will keep warm; But how can one be warm alone? Though one may be overpowered by another, two can withstand him. And a threefold cord is not quickly broken."

Contrary to all the modern cultural relationship debates that start with "I don't need a man" or "What does she bring to the table?" This passage depicts a partnership in which each party adds value to the relationship and covers the shortcomings of the other. In short, together, they are better than they would be alone. Each person's individual impact should contribute to their partner's as well as the couple's overall impact on others. Sometimes, the impact may not be perceptible in the early stages of a relationship, but it can be vividly seen later.

We all know Michelle and Barack Obama from their stay in the White House, but they were not always public or political figures. They were once upon a time both aspiring college students seeking to build successful careers in law. Now, years later, they have impacted the lives of millions of Americans and many more around the world. The position alone placed them into a variety of harsh and unforgiving spotlights, the glare of which could either reveal their facets or expose their flaws. Their contribution to various segments of society was immense. Their very presence gave hope to countless lives around the world.

However, their influence has not ceased since they left the White House. It just continues to be seen in different ways.

Lately, Michelle has carved out a niche as an author and inspirational speaker, among other things. Barack Obama can now weigh in on a variety of issues from a more personal stance and not worry as much about the political ramifications of his words. As I said before, a diamond doesn't cease to be a diamond just because it's no longer in the light. It remains valuable and has the potential to reflect brilliance because of its intrinsic qualities. The same is true of you and your marriage. The purpose for which God allowed you to be joined together in wedlock doesn't change because of the light or the absence thereof. It just becomes more apparent and impactful to others when the light shines on it.

You may not be transitioning from a life in the White House to becoming a regular citizen. But I am confident you have experienced seasons of being scrutinized under the intense light of criticism or judgment. You may have also endured seasons of relative obscurity. You and your spouse may have partnered to do some great things that have been observed by others or not even acknowledged. Regardless of the amount of light and attention, or lack thereof, always remain authentically yourself, so when the light does shine, they see the brilliant you!

Chapter Thirteen

A Brilliant Marriage Requires a Brilliant You

If I could sum up the keys to a brilliant marriage, I would say it boils down to you.

Yes, you.

You - a person who is willing to operate in **covenant.**

You - a person who values constructive **communication**.

You - a person who has clear **core values.**

You - a person who is open to Godly **counsel.**

With all the things that can go right or wrong in human relationships, the only thing we can truly control is ourselves. Ironically, when marriages go bad, both parties typically have a lot to say about what the other person did or did not do. In a divorce proceeding, it is a blame-and-shame game on steroids! However, history has shown that blaming the other party does nothing to solve problems. In fact, it only serves to put the person on the defensive and position them to resist your efforts to get them to change. It may be factually correct to point out your partner's mistakes, messes, hangups, and habits. They may have made bad financial decisions, failed to acknowledge a birthday or anniversary, or made embarrassing comments in public. In their selfishness or cluelessness, they may have minimized your feelings. They may have disrespected your boundaries or eaten the restaurant leftovers you were looking forward to having for lunch. If you haven't figured it out by now, you can't change them. No amount of prodding, begging, cajoling, crying, threatening, or bullying will lead to lasting "heart" change. They may temporarily adjust their behavior to avoid certain consequences, but that might just be temporary. You have no control over their changes. However, you can change yourself!

Marriage brilliance starts and ends with the person who is reading this book. So, your mission, should you choose to accept it, is to bring the brilliance yourself. Stop hoping, praying, and expecting your partner to bring it to you or for you. If you bring as much brilliance to the relationship as possible, you will have done your part to make the marriage brilliant. If you make it your business to allow as much of God's light to shine through you into the relationship, you will have made a life-changing contribution.

Being a Brilliant You!

Being brilliant is not a matter of unleashing some unknown superpowers or doing something spectacular. But it does require some work. This work is a bit different from the work you did to graduate high school, college, or to obtain an advanced degree.

It's different from the work you did to perfect your craft or expertise in your occupation. It's different from the work you did to start and run a successful company. As we noted earlier, many individuals in a marriage relationship are *plenty smart*, *plenty educated*, and *plenty accomplished* on the job or in ministry. Their qualifications look good on paper, but they fail at marriage because it requires a different skill set. Marriage requires the use of a different set of muscles.

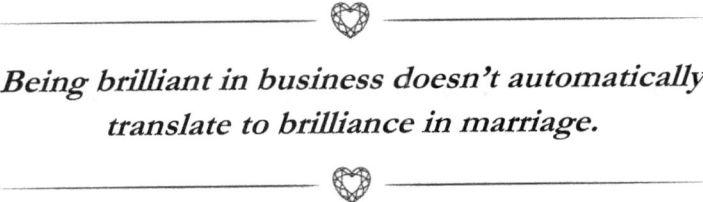

Being brilliant in business doesn't automatically translate to brilliance in marriage.

Being a successful comic in a performance doesn't mean your partner will find you hilarious at home. Being stellar in public doesn't make you shine in private. In many cases, people bring their most brilliant selves to the marketplace and leave their spouses to deal with the duller, unpolished version of themselves. I am not implying that we should act or perform at home. I am not saying we should not be able to express our frustrations or be ourselves at home. What I am saying is that both you and your spouse deserve the best version of each other. Let's look at a few practical things we should be willing to do to bring brilliance to the marriage.

Be Willing to Change

If we are honest, most of us avoid change. I am not just talking about changing jobs or where you live. I am not talking about changing hairstyles. I am talking about changing you! Most people go into marriage feeling like they are good enough the way they are. They figure that since their partner said "I do" at the altar, they were accepting the entire package of facets and flaws. That may be true initially, but as time goes by and different flaws that create relational problems come into view, adjustments and changes need to be made. For example, if one or both parties are careless with money but want to save up for a house, somebody needs to become less careless about money. The added financial responsibility that comes with purchasing and maintaining a home will require changes in their financial priorities and practices. So, in this case, the "single life" habit of spending money on expensive sneakers or designer handbags must be replaced with saving. Intentional budgeting should replace impulsive buying. Why? Because the goals have changed.

I recently realized that I relied on the "I am a nice guy" approach with good intentions way too much. Even when I made glaring mistakes, my fallback position was that I meant well or that I didn't mean anyone any harm. Though my intentions may have been good, the impact of my action (or lack thereof) was not. Relying on my general "nice guy" persona was my way of saying that I don't need to change anything about myself because I am good enough the way I am. It was steeped in pride. It was a quiet resistance to doing what was necessary to get a different outcome in life. It was my way of justifying my position and politely daring anyone to make me change. The realization that change was needed for me or anyone else, however, is just the beginning. The real work is changing a mindset or mentality. For this to happen, it may be necessary to do some work to uncover the origins of why a certain mindset or mentality exists in the first place.

Was your current mindset something that was encouraged or fueled during childhood? Was it a result of a bad experience? Was a personal vow made to be a certain way to combat mommy or daddy issues? We all bring a myriad of behaviors and attitudes into a marriage that we have become accustomed to. They are ours. The problem arises when our partner experiences our behaviors and lets us know that they are not acceptable. A simple example is the single man who routinely goes into the refrigerator and drinks milk or juice directly out of the carton. Nobody but him might know about this habit, and it may be perfectly fine *for him*. But when his new wife sees him do it and proclaims how "nasty" it is, he has a choice to make. He can get defensive. He can conclude that she is calling him a nasty person. He can deride her for challenging his right to do whatever a man wants to do. He can accuse her of stifling his independence. He can decide that she is trying to boss him around again. He can even begin to tell her about all the things she does that he hates. He can conclude that if she is right, he must be wrong, and if he is wrong, then he is a bad person. There are lots of negative ways he could respond to this singular feedback about his actions. Or he can choose to see it another way. He can choose to look past her tone, expression, and body language and see the feedback for what it is. He can attempt to understand what she is communicating. He can give her an opportunity to further explain her concerns. He can see it as her calling the <u>action</u> nasty rather than calling him (the <u>person</u>) nasty. He may agree with her that it is an unsanitary or selfish act. He can see how she might be embarrassed to serve this milk or juice to any thirsty visitors that come into their home. If he is unwilling to change, he will create a whole host of reasons (or excuses) to avoid change. However, if he is willing to change, that will open opportunities for growth and trust in the relationship.

Be Up for the Challenges

Life certainly has enough challenges. Married life challenges, however, hit differently. You are now responsible for thinking about "us," whereas in the past, you only had to think about yourself. It can be a big adjustment for many people. Challenges may come in every conceivable area of life, so I will not attempt to address the multitude of scenarios.

Along with a willingness to change, challenges are designed to stretch and strengthen us. They can also redirect or repurpose us. Along the way, they may expose weaknesses or vulnerabilities. If we manage the challenges properly and together, they can strengthen the relationship in the same way a team that overcomes adversity becomes stronger and more connected. If handled improperly, they can undermine the relationship. Life-changing events such as a chronic illness or physical and mental disability can significantly change the landscape of a marriage. Losing a child or having a special needs child can create incredible strain in a relationship. More common occurrences can include loss of income due to layoffs, losing a home or a business due to a natural disaster, and poor business decisions. None of these events or circumstances are easy to deal with. Just because a couple professes their love for one another does not guarantee they will individually or collectively have the resilience they need to bounce back from adversity.

Many couples do not survive these dire circumstances. Those who do survive do so by deciding to face the challenges head-on. They find creative ways to deal with disabilities. They downsize their lifestyles and rearrange priorities. They relocate or start different careers. They rally around a special needs child and become engaged in causes greater than themselves. They use the memory of a child who died prematurely to fuel their desire to help others through similar pain. They redefine what success looks like for them in their new season. They don't buy into the narrative written by their circumstances. They chose to tell a different story.

They find a way to turn their pain into passion, their losses into lessons, and their tragedies into testimonies and teachable moments.

These are some of the ways that the "fire" of their marriage diamond can be evident in a relationship. These are the glimpses of color that catch the eyes of onlookers who may have thought the marriage should be clouded by crisis. The brilliance of both parties can be seen when they both agree to face the challenges together.

The recent global pandemic became a phenomenon that nobody factored into their *"happily ever after"* marriage journey. The lockdowns, tanking economy, fear of contracting diseases, mask and vaccine mandates, and the sudden loss of friends and loved ones have had a tremendous impact on everyone. Marriages that endured did so under unprecedented stress. When you toss in the constant cycling of news stories on political polarization, vaccine controversies, and social justice issues, along with the national and local death statistics, it becomes difficult to find a place of mental refuge. The strain was apparent in homes where both marriage partners worked remotely in makeshift office spaces.

Both my wife and I worked from home while our two girls (one a college freshman and the other a high school junior) took their classes on Zoom. To add a twist of generational diversity, both my dad and my mother-in-law joined the fray. That's because several months earlier, both had lost their spouses to different forms of cancer. The logical choice was for them to stay with us because we had the space. When the pandemic required us to all stay home, what seemed like adequate space felt limited. So, we were forced to repurpose the space we had. Like everyone else, we couldn't go to the movies on a Friday night, so we took family walks with the dogs. My wife and I tag-teamed in making breakfast for the parents and serving dinner like never before. Where we previously seldom cooked breakfast on weekdays, now we served breakfast as frequently as the local Denny's restaurant. Though the pandemic didn't create dire conditions in our home, it did create new challenges for all of us.

We viewed those challenges as a reason to remodel, repurpose, redefine, redesign, and rearrange several aspects of our daily lives. Thankfully, the changes have served us well, and many of the effects of being locked down are but a memory. I am not sure how long we could have lasted with two seniors, two working adults, two teens, and two dogs in that space! Still, I am glad to say we successfully endured that challenge.

Be a Cheerleader for Your Marriage

I recently married a couple who both had their own individual successes and spotlights. Among the advice I gave them was to treat their new marriage like a baby. I wanted them to realize that even though they knew how to live successfully as individuals before marriage, the new marriage would require feeding, nurturing, and protecting just like an infant. Part of the care for the new marriage would be cheering on every milestone, accomplishment, and achievement they experience together. We have no problem cheering for everything a baby does, from the first poopy diaper to latching onto mom for nursing or taking a bottle. We cheer when they smile and giggle for a photo, grab an object, crawl, and walk for the first time. We show our approval when they recognize colors and shapes, toss a ball, or figure out potty training. I believe the same type of verbal affirmation does wonders for a new marriage. You have both lived your lives individually and quite well. Now it's time to live life together. Now, it's time to succeed together. Now, it's time to seek purpose together. For some couples, this is easier said than done. Going from operating as an individual to operating as a team can take some getting used to. Tendencies to operate as an individual will arise because, often, it's easier or just a matter of habit.

Unfortunately, some people maintain a posture of individuality in their marriages for various reasons. It could be a lingering fear of commitment or an unwillingness to share things they hold dear. Some believe they must sacrifice their individuality if they prioritize the relationship. On the contrary, their individuality creates the dynamic the relationship requires. Cheering for us as a team doesn't mean losing yourself as a person. I have also seen people put up a wall between themselves and their spouses because they claim to hold "family" in high regard. That's because, for them, the "family" they associate with is composed of their mom and/or dad and the siblings they grew up with. They exclude their spouse (typically the wife in my limited experience) from that dynamic. For some men, the mom is more family than the new wife they have a covenant relationship with. I get it. Mom raised you, changed your diapers, and wiped your snotty nose. Mom cooked, cleaned, and gave you unconditional love. As a married man, in your eyes, Mom can do no wrong. Even when the mom attempts to manipulate the son with emotional displays or shows disrespect for your wife to her face, the son will give the mom a pass because she is "family" in his mind. But how, then, does that make the wife feel? It makes her feel like an outsider and anything but family! It makes her feel unsupported. It makes her feel like she is destined to fight for his respect, love, and their marriage all by herself.

This is precisely NOT how to be a cheerleader for your new marriage and potential family. Your family now includes you and your wife as the cornerstone that future generations are going to build upon. This is the family you need to cheer for and make brilliant so the world can see the goodness and glory of God on earth. When he wins, the marriage wins. When she wins, the marriage wins. When we win individually or together, that is a reason to cheer marriage success.

From the traits of a good cheerleader, here are some practical ways you can be a cheerleader in your marriage relationship:

Focus on Team Success

Cheerleaders are specifically there to encourage the team's success. They cheer for both the star player and the player at the end of the bench. Keeping both parties encouraged to do their best for the good of the team is the goal. This applies to your marriage if you are the "star" or the "supporting cast" in the marriage show. Historically, in Western culture, women have been the supporting cast for husbands who make moves in the corporate world. When he got a raise, promotion, or new job, she was often the one celebrating from behind the scenes. However, women are also making marketplace moves these days, from holding down C-Suite positions to leading successful entrepreneurial enterprises. In some cases, the man is the supporting cast for her success. This does not relieve him of his responsibility to provide and protect. But it may shift the financial landscape considerably. If both understand that their individual success is their team's success, they will be on solid ground. However, if it becomes a competition or arms race for marital control, things will deteriorate fast!

Focus on Team Collaboration
Though the cheerleaders encourage the team to perform at its best, they are a team as well. They both must perform together to do their job, like the "flyer" who jumps from the top of a human pyramid or the "anchor" who holds down the bottom of the pyramid. No position is superior or inferior. Collaboration is the key to the cheer team's success. My wife would often utter the phrase "teamwork and specialization" when we worked on a joint project and achieved success. It could be for anything from putting furniture together to folding clothes. The point is that she recognized the value of teamwork and the use of specific skill sets for small and large projects. Could one of us have accomplished the objective individually? In some cases, yes. However, acknowledging our respective roles in any activity served to reinforce the value of collaboration in our relationship.

Focus on Enthusiasm
Nothing is more uninspiring than an unenthusiastic cheerleader! When your partner accomplishes something great, it should be met with some level of interest or enthusiasm. One of the best ways to show enthusiasm is to be vocal. Your joy and elation over

every marriage's success should not be a well-kept secret! If you are proud of their accomplishment, behavior, or actions, they should not have to wonder how you feel. I am not suggesting that you go completely out of character to demonstrate extreme enthusiasm when it's not appropriate. Applauding your husband when he picks up his dirty underwear or finally takes out the trash is unwarranted. To present roses to the wife who finally resists the latest shoe sale is a bit too much. It may also be viewed as sarcasm. However, enthusiastically acknowledging your partner's hard work, perseverance, resolve, or dedication to a project or a cause goes a long way to encourage them and boost their confidence.

Chapter Fourteen

We're in This Together!

I am a firm believer that the energy some couples use in conflict, competition, and combating one another in marriage can be used more productively. For example, when two individuals decide to divorce, they often use their time, energy, and resources to conquer the other party. They end up having complicated communications on how to divide assets, arrange co-parenting routines, and establish new, separate living arrangements. A lot of work is required just to "undo" the marriage they are not happy in! What if all that energy and effort were used to enhance the marriage? What if all that creativity and conniving used to make the other party look like the world's worst parent was used for good and not evil? Either way, they are expending energy and resources to achieve a specific goal. A considerable amount of work had to be done either to remain married or to go their separate ways.

My heart's desire is that couples, young and old, use their individual brilliance to tap into their collective brilliance and put it on display for all the world to see. When the world sees that collective brilliance, they will be blessed and better for it. Your shared brilliance is your gift to the world.

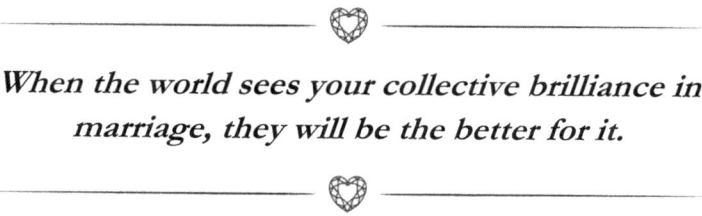

When the world sees your collective brilliance in marriage, they will be the better for it.

There is a popular urban clothing brand that boasts "**Detroit vs. Everybody**" as its motto. According to their website (https://vseverybody.com/), the brand "sought to unite the city of Detroit while politely flipping the bird to the rest of the world." This "us against the world" mantra may come across as a bit offensive to some. However, the intent of founder Tommy Walker was to create "a brand that could rebuild Detroit's image through the restored pride of Detroiters universally." As a result of the campaign, the brand has attained high-profile media coverage and even reached into the world of sports, news, and entertainment. It has caught the attention of a variety of celebrities in the music and entertainment worlds. It has also led to an overflow of copycat artists who want to capitalize on the "**vs. everybody**" theme.

The fuel for the founder's creativity was the unfair media narratives he kept hearing regarding the city of Detroit. He felt it was time to bring attention back to the positive contributions and instill pride rather than focus on the current challenges the city faced. The city of Detroit has a rich culture, including economic enterprises and popular music history. Established in 1701 and incorporated as a city in 1815, it is the largest city in the state of Michigan. Its strong industrial heritage made it fertile ground for the developing automobile industry at the turn of the 20th century. By 1920, the booming industry had propelled Detroit to become the fourth-largest city in the nation. Even though it was badly hit by the Great Depression, it was thriving again by the 1950s and reached its peak population of 1.8 million (about twice the population of Delaware) people. Unfortunately, race riots as early as 1943 and, most significantly, in 1967 have also marred its history. Several factors, including a bankruptcy filing in 2013, led to a decline in its stature. However, since 2014, more money has been invested in city services and infrastructure. Several new commercial opportunities and projects designed to revitalize neighborhoods have been initiated. This does not mean that many of its social problems have disappeared. They have not. But Detroit has been labeled a "renaissance city," considering the work of its cultural and enterprising citizens. Several historical landmarks have been revitalized, repurposed, or reimagined in a way that has attracted new residents and tourists alike.

That is my hope for the institution of marriage and individual marriages. Popular narratives have made marriage out to be a useless institution, simply a piece of paper or a thing of the past. These narratives focus solely on divorce rates, dysfunction, and domestic conflicts to justify why marriage has little to no value in society. Just like the City of Detroit, the institution of marriage has a rich history of contribution and connection to vibrant communities and social stability. Regardless of current social and cultural trends or individual preferences, marriage is the cornerstone of the family.

In God's mind, marriage represents the dynamic relationship between Christ and the church. What we often forget is that Christ certainly suffered pain, humiliation, and loss in demonstrating love for the church. But his pain was the prelude to the resurrection. The church has certainly strayed, struggled, and even staggered at the immense promises of God. His church has been distracted and disgraced by scandals, sometimes of its own making. But His church is not destroyed and has not been discarded by God.

If there is a resurrection for the bridegroom (Christ), surely there is a revival for the bride (the church). In a similar way, there is room for revival in every marriage relationship. Marriages need not be defined or dismissed because of their struggles. Rather, they can be refined through the struggles to become what God calls them to be. That's resilience. They can be polished by pain and still be put on display. That's radiance. In the same way, the challenges Detroit has faced have made it a prime candidate for a renaissance; the challenges of any marriage can be a setup for revival if both parties are open to the possibilities God has in store for them.

We must be willing to embrace and maintain a **covenant** mindset in marriage. We must engage in honest and authentic **communication** with one another. We must remain true to our **core values** and honor the core values of our partner. We must seek godly **counsel** at various stages of the relationship. It is in this setting that the carat, cut, color, and clarity of our marriage diamond can truly reflect the light God shines on it.

So, even if the institution has been challenged over the years, it is not because the institution is flawed. It's because people are deeply flawed and fractured. At the same time, those flawed and fractured people are deeply forgiven by the God who crafted the institution to reflect His brilliance in the world. We don't have to walk around with t-shirts or hoodies that state **"Marriage vs. Everyone"** to politely give the finger to the naysayers. But we do need to take a page from the "Detroit vs. Everybody" book and re-establish the God-ordained "brand" that rebuilds the image of marriage through the restored pride of couples everywhere.

In closing, I want you to take some time to identify the true enemy of your marriage. To help you with this exercise, I will start by stating that it is not your wife or your husband. The **"vs. Everybody"** crew concluded that creating a common outside enemy (namely everybody) served to unify the people of Detroit. The sooner we recognize the "outside forces" that are determined to undermine your marriage, the sooner we can focus our energies appropriately. Who wins when your marriage is not brilliant? Who gains by keeping your marriage relationship looking like a World War II combat zone? Who benefits from you and your partner remaining in the trenches, lobbing grenades of accusation at one another? If you are not sure, let me ask a different question. Who LOSES when your marriage is steeped in conflict, chaos, and confusion? Who loses when you are careless with your words and could care less about keeping your word? Who is victimized when you view your partner as a curse or use curse words to describe them to others?

Here are some observations for your consideration:

Our children *lose* because they do not have a visible pattern to model their marriages after. As they say, more is caught than taught. But if they can't "catch" anything from parents who work through challenges, they will be left to figure out what a healthy marriage looks like by watching reality TV, YouTube influencers, or scrolling through Instagram or TikTok. Rather than learning to fight for something bigger than themselves, they learn to give up, quit, and throw in the towel when their relationships are challenged. It is much easier to "ghost" someone than to go through a process to gain someone's respect. It's easier to evade than to engage. It's easier to criticize and cancel than to challenge someone or communicate real concerns.

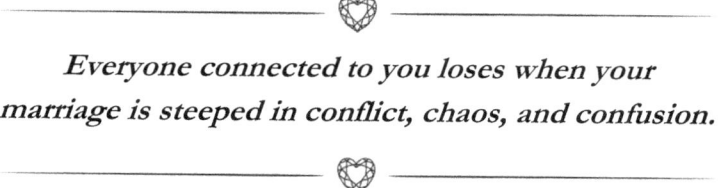

Everyone connected to you loses when your marriage is steeped in conflict, chaos, and confusion.

Our communities *lose* because the relational glue that we are using is not strong enough to keep us together through adversity. Our generation has also embraced "online communities" as a recent reality, driven in part by the recent pandemic. The rise of online and media-driven discussions surrounding the worst aspects of our relationships is staggering. In addition to divorce, we are relentlessly assaulted with talk of people caught cheating, toxic relationships, situational relationships, body counts, the devaluation of men and women, boss chicks, side chicks, gold-diggers, and masculine energy displayed by women. We are told that "high-quality" men can have a side chick if they can afford one, and women may need to lower their personal standards to find or share a man. Men are told they need to be alpha males, that a beta male is not worthy of a "high-quality" woman, and that no man should be a simp. We are lectured on toxic masculinity, deadbeat dads, baby mamas, baby daddies, paternity cases, and a whole host of other relational flashpoints. This keeps us gazing at and glamorizing relational "wreckage" more than relational redemption. Among that wreckage, I stumbled upon a social media broadcast where a 29-year-old male boasted about having seven children by seven different women whom he was not providing child support for. What's worse is that he said the children should not be here because he gave the women the option to abort them, but they chose to keep them. He felt absolutely no remorse for abdicating his paternal responsibility. In fact, he was profiting from his absent father's reputation. We are being inundated with language and images that satisfy our craving to view the sensational, even if it is carnage. We fail to fully realize that it also has the potential to trigger many of the onlookers. I am not suggesting we go back to 1950s values. What I am suggesting is that we take the time to discover and celebrate the beauty and purpose of what God had in mind when he created this thing called marriage.

Our culture *loses* for all the reasons noted above. I have no problem with cultural norms shifting for reasons that advance society. There will always be trends and evolving issues for a variety of groups. Though I come from an unapologetically biblical perspective, I am not interested in thumping a Bible and acting like I am "holier than thou" as I raise these concerns. I am interested in thoughtful dialogue about what serves both our present and future interests. I am interested in evolving while remaining grounded in God's original design and intent for relationships and marriage. I am interested in what is sustainable for our culture – black culture, American culture, and Western culture. We can neither survive nor thrive with an "anything goes" mentality in our relationships.

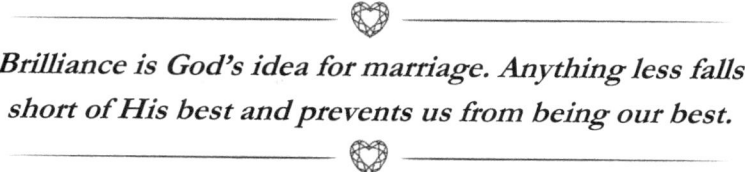

Brilliance is God's idea for marriage. Anything less falls short of His best and prevents us from being our best.

My sincere prayer is that you discover the brilliance your marriage possesses and is called to express. I firmly believe that this brilliance will be on display for all the world to see as you commit to covenant, communication, core values, and counsel as a way of life.

www.ingramcontent.com/pod-product-compliance
Lightning Source LLC
Chambersburg PA
CBHW072155070526
44585CB00015B/1151